The Fifties and Sixties

DERBY

The Fifties and Sixties

Nicola Rippon

north
bridge .co.uk
PUBLISHING

First published in Great Britain in 2014 by

North Bridge Publishing
20 Chain Lane
Mickleover
Derby DE3 9AJ

ISBN 978-0-99267-796-1

Book design by Graham Hales, Derby

Printed and bound by
4edge Limited, 7a Eldon Way Industrial Estate, Hockley, Essex SS5 4AD

Vist the North Bridge Publishing *website for our other local books*
www.northbridgepublishing.co.uk
or search on Amazon for North Bridge Publishing
amazon.com

Selected other books from North Bridge Publishing:
Derby County: Story of A Football Club
Derby Memories
The Day That Derby Won The Cup
When The Rams Met The Nazis
It Happened in Mickleover
Derby: The Thirties and the War Years

Contents

Derby in the Sixties

Introduction

FOR the people of Derby the start of the 1950s brought the first signs that the life they had endured since the end of the Second World War, five years earlier, was beginning to ease. Food and petrol were still rationed and life was still comparatively austere but, little by little, times were changing.

Indeed, by the end of the decade, a new Prime Minister was telling the British that they had "never had it so good". The country was by then well into a new "Elizabethan Age" and in 1953 Derbeians had celebrated the Coronation as much as anyone. Now they looked forward in anticipation of better days to come.

By 1960 life was very different from that at the end of the war. Food was now plentiful, the old restrictions had been largely forgotten, and there was a new "youth culture", the like of which had not before been seen. The austere Fifties were no more; the Swinging Sixties would soon be under way.

In Derby there were plenty of changes, not least to the townscape that, by the end of the decade, had lost some of its much-loved buildings. The town that had survived the war was now beginning to look very different.

Through momentous events – the fires and the floods – and through the minutiae of everyday life – this book reminds us of what it was like to live in Derby in the 1950s and the 1960s.

Anton Rippon
Derby, 2014

Derby in the Fifties

1950

General Election – and an end to petrol rationing

FEWER shortages and reduced rationing, a close-fought General Election, the proposed removal of Derbyshire's seat of government from town to county, a mass Bank Holiday exodus to the countryside and seaside, and the loss of one greatly loved theatrical venue, but the opening of what would become another – the first year of a new decade brought changing times for the people of Derby.

Indeed, 1950 was the year when life in Britain began to return fully to peacetime normality, a year when thoughts could turn to recreation and leisure time with the lifting of many restrictions. First, however, there were serious matters to consider.

The turn of the year saw Derbyshire preparing for a General Election. After Labour's dramatic sweep to power in the euphoric aftermath of VE-Day, recent economic setbacks had brought unpopularity to a government previously lauded for its introduction of the Welfare State.

The three-year "Groundnut Scheme" to plant vast acreages of peanuts in the Tanganyikan bush had failed spectacularly. The scheme was intended both to develop a self-sufficient large-scale mechanised agriculture industry in the African colonies, and to provide resources for making soap and margarine for the hungry British market.

It had cost between £35-£49 million and every penny had been lost. In addition the Attlee Government had been forced to devalue the pound by 30 per cent. The people of Derbyshire, like those in the rest of Britain, were about to voice their dismay.

The result was unrestrained political debate, with no concerns over voter apathy. To ensure his party had the greatest chance of success, Councillor Alec Ling of Derby Conservatives laid on some 40 cars to ferry likely Tory voters from their homes to the polling stations. Councillor Ling, however, believed that most voters were enthusiastic enough to get there under their own steam.

In the run-up to the election, the *Derby Evening Telegraph*'s Derby & Joan column cautioned women to vote for their own choice of candidate. It was a concern echoed by reader Marion Saunders of Hillsway, Littleover, who wrote to the paper in disgust or, as she described it, "feminine rage" because she had overheard a Derby woman complaining bitterly to a friend about the Government, and then sigh: "But my husband always likes me to vote Labour." The appalled Ms Saunders asked: "For heaven's sake, what sort of spineless lot are we that we have to be told how to vote?"

Throughout Election Day, 23 February, the Derby public looked to the latest edition of the *Evening Telegraph* for the relative positions of the parties on what, it was feared, would be a close-run thing. Sure enough, although there were early indications of a comfortable Labour win, by midday it was clear that the final result was unpredictable.

A series of late editions on the 24th brought news of the narrowing gap: in the Late Final, the lead was 19 seats; in two Extra

Special editions it was three and 11 respectively. By Saturday morning, Labour had a lead of just 10 seats, with another six to declare.

With such a close result, it seemed clear that another General Election would soon follow. However, while Britain as a whole had been divided, there was no such uncertainty in Derbyshire with only two constituencies – those of High Peak and West Derbyshire – favouring Conservatives over Labour.

With Labour returned to power in the county, there were widespread fears that it would not be long before a plan to remove the centre of Derbyshire's government from Derby itself would be enacted.

On the day before the election, the Labour group on Derbyshire County Council had confirmed plans to move its headquarters to Matlock. The Borough and County Councils had been at loggerheads over many issues for some time and, with the almost prohibitive estimated cost of building new premises in Derby, the County Council, under the leadership of its chairman, Charles White, preferred the more cost-effective option of purchasing the former Smedley's Hydro, which was more or less ready to move into.

The *Evening Telegraph*, however, predicted "a storm of protest" at the proposal, particularly from residents of Derby. Those of Matlock, it seemed likely, would have less to oppose: the proposed relocation was expected to bring both jobs and investment into the town.

As the annual Whitsun holiday approached, the Minister of Fuel and Power, and MP for Derby South, Philip Noel-Baker, announced an end to petrol rationing. Thanks to two American oil companies which had each promised to import additional supplies to the UK, Noel-Baker declared: "People will be able to buy petrol without coupons and without regard to whether it is white or red". More petrol had been available to commercial vehicles and had been dyed red to prevent its use by private drivers.

Going on holiday – by stagecoach?

NOEL-Baker's announcement meant that, for the first time in many years, those lucky enough to own a car could make the most of the pleasant weather forecast for the Bank Holiday, without worrying about how much petrol they used.

In the north of the county, hotels reported a sudden rush of customers. Garage owners, busy since the announcement, reported brisk trade, although plentiful supplies prevented long queues from forming. Employees at one Derby garage celebrated the end of petrol rationing by bringing out the bunting and flags last seen on VJ Day.

Thousands of Derby folk left the town that day, most bound by car, coach and train for the Peak or the coast. Trains bound for Matlock and Darley Dale were delayed to allow all those queuing in the booking hall to climb aboard, while Derby Bus Station reported large queues for the coaches bound for Skegness, Bridlington, Liverpool and the race meetings at Doncaster and Birmingham.

In Derby itself, locals enjoyed the newly installed miniature railway at Markeaton Park, and the concerts in Darley, Markeaton and Normanton Parks. The star turn, however, was the performance by the famed Black Dyke Mills Band at the Arboretum.

By the time the next Bank Holiday arrived, on 7 August, although there was again a mass exodus from the towns, Britons were becoming used to the novelty of ration-free travel. One Derbyshire man, Darley Dale lead mine director William Smith, renounced motor transport entirely, taking his family on their holiday to Norfolk in his yellow and black stagecoach, pulled by four grey horses. "Car for business, but coach and four for pleasure," declared Mr Smith. It took three and a half days to cover the 150-mile journey at a steady 7mph, but Mr Smith took no chances – included in his party of 11 was blacksmith George Redfern.

The curtain comes down on the Grand Theatre

DECEMBER 1950 marked the last performances at the Grand Theatre on Derby's Babington Lane. Opened in 1886 by impresario Andrew Melville, the original theatre had burned down just six weeks later. But it had been rebuilt, bigger and better, in a matter of months. For 64 years the Grand had staged a wide variety of entertainment and played host to some of the biggest names in British entertainment.

In 1901 the famous actress, renowned beauty and mistress of the Prince of Wales, Lillie Langtry, performed there. She was some years past her heyday and had long been replaced in the affections of the new King Edward VIII, but she was still a famous name. In 1922, Ivor Novello, by then an established film star, appeared in *The Rat*. During the Second World War, many stars, like John Gielgud and Peggy Ashcroft, Anna Neagle and Vivian Leigh, performed in plays that were about to be debuted in London's West End.

As well as dramas, comedies and musicals, variety shows and revues were also staged at the Grand Theatre. Arthur Askey and Vera Lynn were among stars featured; Max Bygraves made his revue debut at the Grand; and Frankie Howerd appeared well down the bill, returning at a later date as the star of the show. Ice shows, water shows and circuses had been held at the Grand.

Despite a substantial redecoration in 1948, the limitations of an old theatre were beginning to tell. There was no way of expanding the Grand's seating capacity, while little could be done to improve general facilities. And the post-war shortage of building materials ruled out erecting a new theatre from scratch.

The nearby Hippodrome on Green Lane became a target for the Grand's proprietor, Prince Littler. Built in 1914, as a Music Hall and Palace of Varieties, the Hippodrome was now being used as a cinema by J Arthur Rank's Circuits Management Association Ltd. Under the agreement that the Hippodrome would not be used as a cinema, Rank agreed to sell the venue to Littler.

But while Derby's theatre patrons might have rubbed their hands together at the prospect of two theatres in the town, Littler had other ideas. He was keen to sell the Grand, but not at the risk of damaging his own trade. Just as the Rank organisation did not want the Hippodrome used to show films, so whoever bought the Grand had to guarantee that it would no longer be used as a theatre.

With the Hippodrome set to open on 23 December, the Grand closed on the 9th of that month, to allow time for stage equipment to be transferred the short distance from Babington Lane to Green Lane. The final company to appear at the Grand were the Ballet Rambert. Their last night performances of *Les Sylphides* and *Peter and the Wolf* were played to a packed house and demand for tickets was so high that there were two potential customers for each available seat. In the third interval, the Mayor of Derby, Alderman Matthew Lowe, addressed the audience, recalling his own memories of the theatre. After the final curtain, the Ballet Rambert's dancer and choreographer, David Paltenghi, made a speech and asked the audience to join him in a rousing, and emotional, rendition of *Auld Lang Syne*.

As Derby's Grand Theatre bid farewell to its last patrons, no new owner had been found and the venue looked set to stand empty for some time to come.

1951

A shopping centre on Eagle Street?

THE seemingly endless schemes for the redevelopment of Derby might be viewed as a 21st-century trend. But as early as 1951, Derby Borough Council had produced their own 20-year proposal for transforming the town into a modern community. And many of those plans have an astonishingly familiar ring about them today.

In 1951, with the whole country caught up in the Festival of Britain, *Evening Telegraph* readers were intrigued to read of proposed improvements to the economic and cultural life of the town.

Many key elements of the scheme will have a familiar sound to modern Derbeians. One in particular proposed changes to the Market Place, which at that time was open to traffic. A new Borough Museum and Art Gallery was planned alongside the existing 18th-century Assembly Rooms. This development would enclose that side of the Market Place. Pedestrian access to Derwent Street would be through a series of arcades beneath the complex in which selections from the Museum's collections could be exhibited. The existing Museum and Art Gallery in the Strand would be taken over by the neighbouring library and an extension to that facility built towards Cheapside.

A new shopping area was proposed along the line of Eagle Street. Fully pedestrianised at its top end at The Spot, it would continue towards the Bus Station on the Morledge and would feature open arcades. A new Market Hall would form part of the development, but little thought had been given to the fate of the existing Victorian Market Hall beside the Market Place.

And a helicopter landing ground by the River Derwent

AN improvement to public transport was also in the minds of Derby's town planners in 1951. With the projected Inner Ring Road would come the removal of the Cattle Market, which would be resited from its traditional location between Bass's Recreation Ground and the end of the Morledge, to the Meadows. This would leave land available to extend the Bus Station and provide a "public service vehicle park".

Rather remarkably, and with an extraordinarily futuristic view of the town, the planners also proposed creating a "helicopter landing ground" on the other side of the Derwent, near Darwin Terrace. This, it was claimed, would be an ideal location with easy access to both the Bus and Railway Stations.

However, the same tract of land was also the target of the Markets Committee which wanted to extend the wholesale market, and of the Post Office which wanted to build a depot there. It was also noted that, between the Bus Station and the Derwent, would be a site that might be "a fine setting for a theatre".

A council house estate for Mackworth

SOME improvements to the town were already under way. A large deficit in housing had created very long waiting lists for local authority-owned rented property, and a large building project was already in progress. In May, the first council house on the new Mackworth Estate was completed. Eventually expected to comprise some 2,800 homes and house an estimated 10,000 people, the Mackworth Estate, with its street names given a London theme, was among the first in the country to be built on a "neighbourhood unit" plan. Number 1 Enfield Road, a three-bedroomed home, was officially opened by the Mayor, Alderman Matthew Lowe, who was joined by Mr and Mrs P. Wright who were very much looking forward to moving in with their eight-month-old son, Martin.

Despite this, early returns from the 1951 census revealed that the population of Derby had actually declined by some 1,256 people over the previous 20 years, yet the county had seen an increase in population. Much of this was due to an increasing number of housing estates being built near to, but just outside, the borough boundary.

Bus fares increased – and energy must be saved

WHILE local issues were a welcome distraction, political instability was something of which everyone was still aware. Following the previous year's close-run General Election, another election was called in October. Although the weather was unpleasantly damp and foggy, and it had been only a matter of months since the previous ballot – and even less time since the local elections – the *Evening Telegraph* reported "a steady stream to the polls", with many polling station across the country reporting queues as voting opened.

This time, the Conservatives were the victors, giving Winston Churchill the opportunity to form his first peacetime administration. However, political analysts warned that another narrow victory might well necessitate yet another General Election before too long.

Post-war austerity and a reduction in manpower had meant that now that industry was getting back on track, the production of coal could not keep pace with the huge increase in demand,. While domestic customers were being encouraged to save energy wherever possible, it was industry that felt the brunt of the shortage. Mr C. R. King, chairman of the East Midlands Electricity Board, addressing a fuel efficiency conference organised by the Ministry of Fuel and Power in Leicester, recommended that every factory and business should employ a "fuel watcher" to ensure that no energy was being wasted.

Mr King warned that all machinery, large and small, should be shut off when not in use, and employers should encourage care from its employees. Homeowners should also take care not to waste energy. Sir Herbert Houldsworth, chairman of the East Midlands Divisional Coal Board, agreed. "We cannot get through our difficulties by putting the burden on the other fellow. All must help," he warned.

Derbeians were also dismayed to learn that bus fares were likely to rise. In January, the Borough Council, concerned with a budget deficit, requested permission to increase fares on its petrol and trolley buses. This had been followed in February by an announcement by the town's other major bus company, Trent, that it was about to increase its fares across the board.

Fares of between 1d and 2½d were to increase by 1½d, while those between 3s 9d and 3s 11d would increase by 5d. This was the first time in the company's history that a general fare increase had been implemented. The rise had, the company assured its customers, been considered only "after fighting a desperate but losing battle against ever increasing costs". Rises in the cost of buses and their maintenance, and a national increase in bus drivers' and conductors' wages, were blamed.

Two days later, the *Evening Telegraph* announced that the Borough Council had discovered that the fare increases it had requested would not cover the rising costs; the council reapplied for even greater increases.

Derby's young stars of stage and screen

ON a happier note, the *Evening Telegraph* reported the adventures of one of the county's most promising young stars. In February, Derby-born actress, Joan Rice, celebrated her 21st birthday by attending the London premiere of her film *Blackmailed*. Playing Alma, an artist's model, she appeared alongside Mai Zetterling and Dirk Bogarde. A few days earlier, the beauty had signed a two-year contract with the J Arthur Rank organisation. The *Evening Telegraph* noted: "Yet two years ago, she was a domestic servant in Nottingham." Back in Derby, young Sunderland-born James Bolam was beginning his training as a chartered accountant with Lings in the Wardwick. A former Bemrose School pupil, Bolam was a keen actor, having been involved with many drama productions at the grammar school. One day, like Rice, he would become a household name beginning with the BBC TV series *The Likely Lads*.

Another Derbeian to be hitting the headlines was composer and arranger Ronald Binge, whose lovely arrangement of *Charmaine* was propelling Mantovani to international fame. Less well known, both for his work and his Derby connections, was character actor Frank Conroy. Born in Hayworth Street in

Derby in 1890, the former Burton Road resident had emigrated to the United States and found plentiful work in Hollywood. In 1951, he featured in the thought-provoking science fiction film *The Day the Earth Stood Still*, playing a diplomat.

Despite the seemingly endless shortages they endured, with bold plans for the future, and the successes of its sons and daughters, the people of Derbyshire were beginning to look forward.

1952

The King is dead ...

FOR Derbyshire, as for the whole of Britain, 1952 was a year dominated by the death of a much-loved king, and by the accession of his young daughter. Although the nation knew that their monarch was not in good health – he had appeared unwell during the traditional Christmas broadcast only six weeks earlier, and had looked tired and drawn as he waved goodbye to his daughter and her husband when they left London Airport at the start of their long Commonwealth tour just seven days before – the suddenness of his death came as a shock.

When the simple announcement came from Sandringham House, at 10.45 on the morning of Wednesday, 6 February, a stunned nation learned that, after a sudden decline overnight, King George VI had died in his sleep. Among the first to hear the sombre news were thousands of Derbyshire children listening to a schools broadcast on the BBC wireless service. Even the eight and nine-year-olds in the class, children normally too young to fully appreciate a world event, were shocked by the words they heard.

The king was held in great affection by the British people who he had led through some of the darkest days in the country's history. He had never wanted, nor indeed expected, to be king, but had fought against acute shyness and a speech impediment to accept his duty following the abdication of his brother, Edward VIII, later the Duke of Windsor.

One Derby woman summed up most people's feelings when she told a newspaper reporter: "I feel quite stunned." And one Derbyshire man had special reason to be devastated by the king's death. Tom Jerram, the eldest son of Mr and Mrs Jerram of 35 High Street, Chellaston, had been the king's personal valet for more than 25 years.

Some comfort from private grief was given in the public rituals and ceremonies that took place over the next few days. At 11am on Friday, 8 February, as the public proclamation of the Queen's accession was made at St James's Palace, the Mayor of Derby, Councillor Zachariah Padgin Grayson, read the same statement from the steps of the Council House and, for the first time in their lives, hundreds of people joined in singing the unfamiliar *God Save the Queen*.

A fanfare of trumpets heralded the proclamation and, afterwards, some of the crowd moved on to the County Hall in St Mary's Gate where the High Sheriff of Derbyshire, Mr G. C. M. Jackson, read again the proclamation, this time on behalf of the county.

Many scheduled events had to be postponed or cancelled. Major J. W. Chandos-Pole, presiding at the Derbyshire Conservative Political Club lunch at Ramsden's Cafe in the Cornmarket, asked members to stand in silence, and an address by Peter Bailey, chairman of the Conservative Association's East Midlands Area Education Committee, was cancelled. Derby Borough Police's rugby match against Monmouthshire Police was also cancelled, as was a dance that was to have followed at the Borough Police Station. The regular midweek meeting at Derby's greyhound stadium was called off, as was the annual dinner and dance of Derby Chamber of Trade, to have been held at the old Assembly Rooms.

There was some controversy, however, when the Rialto Ballroom announced that dancing would still be held there. Proprietor Mr J. Aldread explained: "It's a Forces invitation dance and I can't cancel it at such short notice." While the Derby public were prepared to accept that Mr Aldread had been placed in a difficult position, they were less convinced by Sam Ramsden, who announced that his dance night at the Plaza the following evening would also have to go on "because I'm under contract with a Birmingham band".

His decision brought intense criticism and several angry letters to the *Derby Evening Telegraph*.

Many Derbeians made the journey to London to see the King's lying-in-state at Westminster Hall. One Derbyshire-born man, warmed only by a black overcoat and an oil heater, was hard at work producing a painting of the lying-in-state. Frank Beresford, who had studied at Derby School of Art at the end of the 19th century, had performed the same service 16 years earlier at the lying-in-state of George V.

Meanwhile, work continued in Derby on the Borough's funeral wreath. Produced by T. Rowley & Sons, the wreath measured five feet in diameter and proved too large to be assembled at the florist's Green Lane premises. After completion it was displayed at the Council House and a steady stream of Derby people filed past it.

On the day of the funeral, Derby held its own civic procession and memorial service at the Cathedral to coincide with events in London. Two minutes' silence was held across the town, signalled by the sounding of the air-raid sirens at 2 pm. Men, women and children in homes, schools, factories, offices, shops, and in the streets, stopped what they were doing, removed their hats and bowed their heads to pay their personal tribute. As the rumble of traffic died, the procession began its sombre journey from Corporation Street to the Cathedral, accompanied by the strains of Handel's Dead March from Saul. The only other sounds

Charles Stone VC, the Ripley-born war hero who died in 1952.

audible: the faint whispers of mourners, the crisp steps of the marching feet, and the Cathedral's minute bell.

All across Derbyshire, similar services and memorials were in progress, the people of a county, and of a nation, united in grief for their dead king.

1952 also marked the death of Ripley-born Charles Stone VC at the age of 63. He had won the nation's highest honour for courage in 1918, during the Germans' spring offensive France, and had later won the Military Medal before returning to civilian life, and employment at Rolls-Royce. A special memorial service was held in his honour at Belper British Legion

A narrow escape from tragedy

THERE were near escapes from tragedy as a Rolls-Royce party of 520 people from Derby, Burton, Belper and Ilkeston were witnesses to a terrible accident at the Farnborough Air Show in September 1952.

Some 130,000 pairs of eyes were on a de Havilland 110 fighter as tragedy struck. The aircraft made its approach, breaking the speed of sound and producing a sonic boom to great excitement and applause. But on its second, low-level, pass, as the aircraft travelled at speeds of around 500mph, its nose lifted slightly and the plane disintegrated.

Mrs H. G. Pick of Enfield Road, Kingsway, told the *Evening Telegraph*: "Suddenly streams of smoke left it as though it were firing rockets. The body started to fall to earth and the engines hurtled over our heads, landing about 50 yards away." As one of the engines fell on to waste ground, the other plunged into a crowd on a hillside and the rest of the plane, including large pieces of the cockpit, was hurled to earth causing death, injury and destruction on a huge scale.

There was panic as spectators tried to locate their colleagues and loved ones. At least one young woman from the Rolls-Royce party had her eye blackened and her cheek cut by pieces of the plane's fuselage. But, like Gilbert Ford of Buchan Street, Derby, she could later reflect on her good fortune. "It was all so sudden and tragic," Mr Ford told the *Telegraph*.

The days that followed revealed the full extent of the disaster. Only yards away from the Rolls-Royce party some 31 people had been killed and dozens more had suffered serious injury.

A new theatre for Derby

WHILE the shadow of tragedy hung heavily over much of the year, several Derbeians celebrated success. Normanton's Herbert Beetham appeared in his third English billiards championships final, while young actress Joan Rice, who spent her early childhood in Abbey Street, was propelled to stardom in Walt Disney's *The Story of Robin Hood and His Merrie Men*, playing Maid Marion opposite Richard Todd's Robin Hood. Meanwhile home-style guru and florist of choice for society hostesses, Constance Spry – who was born in Warner Street, later lived in Wilson Street, and had provided the flowers for the wedding of Princess Elizabeth – published her book *How To Do The Flowers*.

And there were new beginnings, too, as the Derby Playhouse welcomed audiences for the first time to its premises in the former Baptist Chapel on Sacheverel Street. Unlike its predecessor, the Little Theatre in Becket Street, the Playhouse, with its permanent repertory company, was to stage only professional productions.

Despite all the sadness of 1952, Derbyshire, like the nation around it, seemed to be finally pulling away from the dark days of the first half of the 20th century, and looking forward to a new year and a new "Elizabethan Age".

1953

Power station for Willington – and a new school for Littleover

THROUGHOUT the nation, 1953 was inevitably dominated by the coronation of Britain's new young queen, Elizabeth II. But before Derbyshire could join in the celebrations, there were some important local issues to be considered – not least the official opening of one new school, and, a few miles up the road, the lobby organised by another, ancient, educational establishment against what was to become a familiar sight in the latter half of the 20th century.

In late May, an enquiry was under way into objections against the building of a new power station at Willington. The loudest voices raised against the plan came, surprisingly, not from the residents of the villages to the south-west of Derby, but from the governors of Repton School.

Their representative, Eric Blain, said that Repton, founded in 1557, had become one of England's "really great public schools" and that parents, who chose such a school for its "healthy rural surroundings", might be tempted to go elsewhere by "half a dozen cooling towers and industrial buildings". The governors requested that the power station be built at least one mile from the school.

Meanwhile, as Littleover Secondary Modern on Pastures Hill, celebrated its official opening, one of the visiting dignitaries caused a stir by pointing out that the premises were already something of an anachronism.

School designers had now decided that schools should be built upwards, in towers, rather than stretched out over a large site. But the pupils and teachers, who had been using Littleover School since 1949, were more than pleased with both the facilities and buildings.

Land for the school had been purchased in 1936, but work had not begun until after the Second World War. The style, if a little functional, was elegant enough and featured several nods to the still fashionable art moderne design. Two long corridors stretched outwards from a central entrance hall, with two further corridors running off each of them.

And, while a gymnasium block had yet to be built, hard tennis and netball courts, playing fields, two football pitches, two hockey pitches and a cricket square had all been incorporated, as had an assembly hall featuring a theatrical stage with lights, a green room and a dressing room.

Between two of the classrooms had been built a 'flatlet', comprising kitchen, bathroom and living room, for girls to practise housekeeping.

Long live the Queen ...

BUT it was the crowning of Elizabeth II on Tuesday, 2 June that occupied almost everyone. By the end of May, the county's Coronation celebrations were well under way.

The biggest in Derby – the Derby and County Coronation Year Exhibition – was held on Bass's Recreation Ground from 29 May until 13 June. Some 400 stands were erected, staffed by 1,500 people representing organisations and businesses of all descriptions, including Rolls-Royce and British Celanese, who presented their 'Court of Fashion'.

This featured beautiful creations by top designers of the day, including Norman Hartnell, who, six years earlier, had designed the new queen's wedding dress, all made from Celanese fabrics. The exhibition enjoyed an average daily attendance of 7,000 and several local businesses reported making important overseas trading contacts.

Derbyshire had its own representatives in the official Coronation celebrations, too. Derby-born Constance Spry was commissioned to decorate Westminster Abbey for the ceremony and, with her creative and business partner, Rosemary Hume, invented a cold buffet dish – Coronation Chicken.

Littleover's Stan Bellaby, a 22-year-old lance-sergeant in the Queen's Company, Grenadier Guards, was one of those chosen to mount guard over the crown and coronation regalia. The former Derby Co-operative Society employee was due to be demobbed the following month, after five years' service in the Grenadiers and looked forward to joining Derbyshire County Police.

Many years later, now retired from the police and living in Ripley, Stan Bellaby recalled that great day: "A temporary annex had been built on to Westminster Abbey, to be used by various dignitaries to get ready before entering the Abbey itself. We stood shoulder to shoulder around the edge of the room, with rifles and bayonets and no room to move. I recognised many faces from newspaper photographs. The one that still stick in my mind is Winston Churchill, who was within touching distance of me."

Another local man serving in the Grenadier Guards, 20-year-old Lawrence Lambert, whose family lived at Lord Street, Allenton, would be in the Coronation procession, and 21-old Musician Eric Beardsall, from Allen Street, Allenton, would be playing the euphonium in the Royal Naval School of Music Band in the procession, while yet another Derby representative would be 19-year-old Daniel Docherty of Brackens Lane, Alvaston, who was one of the Irish Guardsman chosen to line the route.

In Derby, official celebrations began the day before the Coronation, with schools closing at Monday lunchtime until Wednesday morning, the exception being the town's grammar schools where examinations meant that pupils would have only Coronation Day off. That Monday morning, some 23,000 Derby children received an inscribed spoon from the Education Authority and at each school an appropriate ceremony was held "to bring home to the children the meaning and significance of the Coronation".

Meanwhile, the peace of the Riverside Gardens was broken by two loud explosions from across the Derwent, near Exeter flats, where armoured cars of the Derbyshire Yeomanry were practising the 21-gun salute they were due to give at 10.26am on Coronation Day, at the exact moment the Queen would leave Buckingham Palace on her way to Westminster Abbey.

The cold and damp Coronation Day weather did its best to bedraggle the bright bunting that decorated most of the county's streets, but did little to dampen spirits. Those lucky enough to own televisions threw open their doors to neighbours, who gathered around the tiny, flickering black and white screens for hours on end. Many others saw the ceremony on televisions in a large tent at Bass's Rec.

The inclement weather conditions caused the cancellation of some events. The fireworks display at Markeaton Park was one – a display held the previous Saturday had attracted 2,000 people who saw an image of the Queen's face surmounted by a crown outlined in white and yellow fireworks – while at Normanton Park, the Sherwood Foresters Band played as scheduled and the Middies managed a display of counter-marching before the rest of the programme was cancelled.

The fair at the Racecourse did a little better, with a steady stream of children enjoying the rides and sideshows, while local cricketers struggled gamely through their tournament in weather more suitable for football. Not surprisingly, considering that most of the exhibits were indoors, events on Bass's Rec attracted by far the most visitors.

In Derby there were nearly 250 street parties. The Town Council had allocated 12 guineas (£12.60) as prizes to be awarded to the three best-decorated streets in the borough. The residents of Grey Street, off Gerard Street, won first prize. Tubs containing masses of flowers were set at regular intervals on the pavements down either side of the street, every window sill had a window box filled with red, white and blue flowers, and at the bottom of the street, a large board proclaimed: "God Save The Queen," while naval signal flags spelled out the same message.

The mayoress received a bouquet from five-year-old Valerie Wood, whose parents had organised the decorations and who themselves were presented with a "hall set" by grateful neighbours.

Tewkesbury Street and Gisborne Street tied for second place, and there were commendations for Winchester Crescent, Colombo Street, Norman Street, Birdwood Street, Harcourt Street, St Luke's Street, York Street, Bath Street, Albion Street, Canal Street and Nelson Street.

Almost every street leading from London Road, between The Spot and Bateman Street, held a party, and many forms of alternative accommodation were negotiated in a bid to beat the elements as schoolrooms, garages, cycle sheds and the spare rooms behind pubs were utilised. Yates Street celebrated beneath a "God Save the Queen" banner some 116 years old; it had hung over the same street on Queen Victoria's Coronation Day in 1837.

While many parties were forced indoors because of the weather, 60 children from Osmaston Road refused to be daunted and donned raincoats to eat their tea in the open. In Harrison Street, too, scores of children ignored the rain and insisted on enjoying their tea in the street as planned.

Residents of Underhill Avenue had also managed their tea and were about to embark on their sports when the rain came down again. There was a brief interval while mothers went to fetch raincoats and wellington boots, and then the festivities continued, although the participants in the ladies versus gents cricket match got thoroughly soaked.

Many communities arranged their own fancy dress competition: in Etwall Street, one up-to-the-minute costume was that of a mountaineer, a tribute to the first successful attempt on Mount Everest, which had been announced earlier that day.

For several families Coronation Day was marked by a new arrival. Mr and Mrs Geoffrey Ellis celebrated the birth of a baby son, while Mrs Kathleen Storer welcomed her daughter, Elizabeth June. Other Coronation Day babies included a daughter to Mrs Betty Jackson, born at home in Curzon Lane, Alvaston; Elizabeth Danuta Wasikowska and Jill Bennett were born at the Queen Mary Maternity Home, while six babies – Hans Peter Foss, Neville William Hollies, Sarah Sherbrook, Michael Robert Poole, Philip John Hunkin, and Donald William Holmes – were born at the Nightingale Maternity Home. At the City Hospital, one boy – Anthony John Dakin – and one girl – Elizabeth Mary Snuggs – also made their entrance.

Two weeks after the Coronation, there was an additional treat for 13,000 children from town and county who attended local cinemas to see film of the glorious event. The Gaumont on London Road showed both a newsreel and a 90-minute Technicolor film entitled *A Queen is Crowned*, which was narrated by Sir Laurence Olivier. Audiences at the Odeon in St Peter's Street and the Regal in East Street were treated to *Elizabeth is Queen*, a newsreel and a film about Westminster Abbey.

For many, the Coronation celebrations seemed to mark the end of post-war austerity in Britain and a new hope for the future. As the year drew to a close, the people of Derbyshire looked forward, with enthusiasm.

1954

Market charter celebrations

IF the Coronation of Queen Elizabeth II already seemed a distant memory, 1954 provided plenty of opportunities for the people of Derbyshire to celebrate, even if the weather seemed determined to scupper every occasion.

The year began with snow and ferocious winds, followed by heavy rains, which almost caused the Derwent to breach its banks as far downstream as Derby. The freezing weather continued into February, as lakes froze over amid warnings not to venture on to the ice in the treacherous conditions. Summer fared little better, with the county suffering the wettest June for 98 years, causing the *Derby Evening Telegraph* to declare: "Never was rain so continuous or unpredictable." September, however, brought some relief with Derbyshire basking in late summer sunshine, with temperatures that reached well into the 80s. This was especially fortunate for the people of Derby, who were about to celebrate one of the biggest festivals in the town's modern history.

The brainchild of the Mayor of Derby, Alderman Alec Ling, the "Octocentenary" celebrations marked 800 years of Derby's history since Henry II granted a market and fairs charter. The precise date of the charter was unclear, but Alderman Ling chose to fix the date to the first year of Henry's reign – 1154 – and the people of Derby joined in enthusiastically. All manner of events were organised, including a dinner-ball for 450 special guests in a "monster" marquee at Markeaton Park. The main event, though, was a huge pageant, the "Civic Cavalcade", which was witnessed by thousands of excited Derbeians. The parade route stretched from Bass's Recreation Ground to Markeaton Park, and was led by the bands of the Borough Police and the Sherwood Foresters. Many local businesses and organisations took part, decorating dozens of colourful floats which were paraded through the town. Derby Borough Fire Service exhibited no less than 10 appliances representing 200 years of firefighting, while the firemen joined in by wearing historical uniforms. The Borough Police also had its officers dressed in old-fashioned costumes and an old horse-drawn tram paraded alongside a modern diesel-engined bus that had only just entered service. Other less glamorous, but no less important, elements of daily life were also represented. A horse-

The Mayor of Derby, Alderman Alec Ling, waves to the crowd who are watching the 1954 carnival parade that celebrated the granting of a market charter to Derby.

drawn street sweeping machine paraded alongside "this year's model, which collects the dust as it sweeps". George Fletcher & Co Ltd displayed sugar machinery and staff of the Co-operative Society donned historical dress to depict Henry II and his court. At Markeaton Park, a whole sheep was roasted, and Derbeians took full advantage of the lifting of wartime food rationing only three months earlier.

Sadly, 1954 marked the closure of one of Derby's favourite meeting places. The Jacobean Café had opened in the inter-war years in the 17th-century house on the Wardwick, once occupied by John Gisborne, the town's mayor.

Post-war boom for local industry

MANY Derby businesses were enjoying a post-war boom in 1954. Rolls-Royce was proud to showcase their new engine – the

Avon RA28 gas turbine, which would soon be used by a new generation of aircraft.

Behind-the-scenes, the engineering firm were also involved in top-secret work. They were instrumental in the development of the Thrust Measuring Rig, or "flying bedstead" as it became affectionately known. A steel framework was mounted on legs with castors for wheels and had two Nene turbojet engines attached, so that the engines' output was directed downwards. The purpose of this was to test how successfully jet engines could lift an aircraft or apparatus, and how easily such an invention could be controlled.

While much of the advanced testing for this took place in Hucknall, the Derby factory was also closely involved in another classified project. Blue Streak, which was in its infancy in 1954, was initiated to produce a jet rocket capable of delivering an unmanned nuclear weapon from Britain into the Soviet Union because the RAF's aircraft were considered too vulnerable to Russian air defences. More publicly, Field Marshall Viscount Montgomery, who was on his way to inspect Repton School's cadet force, toured Rolls-Royce factories.

The *Evening Telegraph* was delighted to report that most of the county's industries were faring well. In Derby, unemployment stood at only 0.4 per cent of the insured population, and many businesses were expanding or preparing to relocate to new industrial estates like those at Raynesway, and on the site of the former Osmaston Park, where the Ascot Drive complex had sprung up.

Royal Crown Derby reported a record year, and increased its staff from 500 to 600 employees. And confectionary manufacturers, Nestle, were in negotiations to build a new factory on a 15-acre site on the outskirts of Mickleover.

Sporting ups and downs

DERBYSHIRE sport had its ups and downs in 1954. For Derby County there had already been the indignity of relegation from the old First Division in 1953, and a bad start to the 1954-55 season would ultimately result in another relegation and Third Division football for the first time in the Rams' history.

Local cricket fans enjoyed a more successful year – and yet still had reason to be disappointed. Derbyshire CCC were robbed of what would have been only their second County Championship, when rain denied them a chance to finish their last, and critical, game. Their rivals, Surrey and Yorkshire, both won their games and Derbyshire had to settle for third place.

There was also a Derbyshire accent to the most memorable sporting moment of the year – Roger Bannister's first sub-four minute mile. Third in the race at Oxford's Iffley Road was Tibshelf miner and rat catcher Tom Hulatt. It was Hulatt's first selection for the AAA team in a meeting against Oxford University on 6 May, and came as something of a surprise to the athletics fraternity.

Although Hulatt's strong position and excellent record – he was Derbyshire and Northern Counties one-mile champion, and one of the most talented middle-distance runners in the country – proved he was undoubtedly an athlete of some excellence, and certainly worthy of selection, the other five runners were all Oxbridge men from middle-class backgrounds, while Hulatt had once had to sleep rough the night before a meeting because he could not afford overnight accommodation.

There were suggestions that his inclusion was to divert attention from a staged record attempt. The previous year Bannister had had one record wiped from the record books due to suspicions of pacemaking – then not, as today, an acceptable method of record-breaking. Hulatt's part in the race somewhat eased such suspicions – officially at least. In the dressing room, however, there was no doubt that a record attempt was being planned and Bannister, Chris Brasher and Chris Chataway, the latter pair both accomplished athletes in their own right, were quite open about their strategy. Hulatt would later tell the *Sunday Express*: "I knew the record attempt was on because Bannister asked me to keep out of his way on the first two laps."

But the decision to go ahead with the attempt came only at the last moment – unfriendly weather conditions had threatened and only shortly before the race had the winds eased. After a false start, Brasher took off from the gun at a blistering pace, closely followed by Bannister and Chataway, while the rest of the runners trailed behind. As Brasher tired, Chataway took up the pace before finally, just 300 yards from the finish line, Bannister made a break for the front. As he crossed the line in a time of 3 minutes, 59.4 seconds, Tom Hulatt was some distance behind, but content to be running his own race. He finished in a very creditable time of 4 minutes 16 seconds.

While the media frenzy surrounded Bannister, Hulatt, despite his third-place, was largely ignored. After obtaining Bannister's autograph, he and his brother repaired to a pub and, after a pint and a sandwich, caught a train back to Derbyshire. Although was never again selected for the AAA, Hulatt retained nothing but fond memories of the experience. "It was an exhilarating night and I was proud to have taken part in such a historic race."

Bemrose School's dramatic talent

DERBYSHIRE also had plenty to boast about in the entertainment industry. Derby-born starlet, Joan Rice, starred in two films: with Burt Lancaster in *His Majesty O'Keefe* and as Iris in *One Good Turn*, helping Norman Wisdom to save an orphanage from closure, in one of the funnyman's finest films.

Meanwhile, another Derby actor, Eric Lander, appeared in a small role in *The Colditz Story*. At Lander's former grammar school, Bemrose, headmaster Eric Bennett praised the dramatic talents of another pupil. Michael Knowles, who would go on to star in numerous television sitcoms, most notably *It Ain't 'Arf Hot Mum!* and *You Rang, M'Lord?*. Knowles had just completed his school career with the lead role in the school's production of

Henry V and had earned rave reviews: "He carried the play on his shoulders ... dominating every scene ... a fine performance, a fitting climax to a very successful career in school drama," enthused one critic.

Civic dramas on an unprecedented scale

THE year was also full of what the *Derby Evening Telegraph* called "civic dramas of unprecedented duration and scale". To the south of the county, the River Dove Water Scheme was officially approved at governmental level. This enabled the building of a new reservoir near Staunton Harold Hall, which would flood some 170 acres of land and submerge farms, like Calke Mill Farm, New England Farm and Furniss Farm, as well as several cottages including an 18th-century lodge to nearby Calke Abbey.

The ongoing plans to convert Smedley's Hydro at Matlock into a new county hall also continued to prove controversial. The County Council claimed it could save £100,000 if it were allowed to move from Derby but, amid objections from many quarters, a three-day public enquiry was held in September to consider the proposal.

Derby Borough Council, meanwhile, was having more luck with its new premises. After a decade of delay, the council's new debating chamber at the Council House was ready for use. On 21 October 1954, the last meeting at the Guildhall was adjourned and the council resumed in its new home. There was much to look forward to as 1955 dawned.

1955

A new era of economic growth

AS 1955 dawned, the *Derby Evening Telegraph* was heralding a new era of economic stability and growth. "Industrial Derby," it declared, "is entering a new phase of tremendous possibilities."

By 1954, Derby County had installed floodlights at the Baseball Ground and were trying them out with a series of friendly matches.

More woe for Derby County

IF industry was prospering, quite the opposite could be said of the town's most important distraction from the working week. Derby County ended the 1954-55 season with relegation to the Third Division North, for the first time in the club's history, drawing to a close an era of buoyancy that had followed the club's victory in the first post-war Cup Final.

Indeed, so poorly were the Rams faring that the directors, fearful that a fixture clash with Derbyshire County Cricket Club would affect their attendance, postponed the kick-off of the Rams' match against Mansfield Town – the first fixture of the 1955-56 season – to the evening.

Then, in December, came ignominy as the Rams crashed out of the FA Cup in the second round at the hands of Midland League side, Boston United. In what was certainly one of the greatest shocks in the competition's history, Boston scored six goals to the Rams' one.

Adding insult to injury, no less than six former Rams players, among them Cup-winner Reg Harrison who had left the Baseball Ground only six months earlier, took the field for the Fenland team, who were managed by another ex-Rams player, Ray Middleton.

Derby County did recover, eventually narrowly missing out on promotion, while Derbyshire's cricketers, hindered by an injury to fast bowler Les Jackson, finished only eighth in the County Championship after a promising start, and much expectation, raised by their successes of the previous season, when at one time they looked likely to win the title.

For one former Rams player, a new life beckoned. Ex-England full-back and Chester Green native, Bert Mozley, and his wife, Jean, herself a Derby girl, had decided to emigrate to Canada with their daughters, Lynne and Lea. In January 1955, Bert had gone ahead to prepare the way. After a long sailing he landed in Nova Scotia and after a three-day railway journey arrived in the Mozleys' new home in Calgary. Fifty-nine years later, they are still living happily in Canada.

Closer to home, snooker and billiards star Joe Davies, a native of Whitwell in the north of the county, made history by recording the first recognised maximum break of 147.

"He struck the headmaster two savage blows ... "

FOR Bemrose School headmaster Eric Bennett there were greater concerns than sporting records. At the school's speech day he told his audience that he had made enquiries among the Bemrose fifth form and discovered that half the form had television sets at home and were spending on average one and a half hours every evening watching the set. He accepted that "some of the programmes may well have an educational value" but felt that "nevertheless, television is a supine affair". For another headmaster in the county, it was pupils' behaviour, rather than academic achievement, which preoccupied him. A report in the *Daily Mirror*, which that year was making something of an issue out of the rights and wrongs of corporal punishment, reported a trial at Heanor magistrates' court in which a 14-year-old schoolboy, from an unnamed school, was accused of assaulting his headmaster as the head tried to administer a caning.

The headmaster was "was about to use the cane when the boy rushed at him and grabbed it," stated the prosecution, "He struck the headmaster two savage blows in the face and kicked him. When the headmaster sat down, the boy hit him twice on the head and then ran away."

As if that ordeal was not enough, the boy's mother later arrived at the school to confront the teacher, and several days later his sister entered his office and threw papers and files around the room, and even pelted the headmaster himself.

The court fined the mother £3 for assault and £4 for behaving in a disorderly manner. Her daughter was fined £5 for assault and £5 for disorderly behaviour, and later the Heanor juvenile court fined the boy £3 for assault.

Spies, the Nobel Prize and a renegade socialite

THE errant pupil from Heanor was not the only Derbyshire native whose behaviour made national headlines in 1955.

Derby-born socialite Lady Norah Docker happily admitted to *Life* magazine that she had assaulted an employee of the casino in Monte Carlo.

"It was a good sock I gave that man, and he deserved it," she told the magazine.

Never far from the gossip columns, she had earlier that year been spotted arriving in typically decadent style for a marbles match between the team from her millionaire husband's British Small Arms factory and a Castleford factory girls' team: the entire away team was driven to the match in Lady Docker's zebra fur-lined, gold-plated Daimler. At Ascot races, Lady Docker received a more favourable press for her wide-brimmed hat, lace suit and mink stole.

The year 1955 was an important one in the careers of several entertainers with Derbyshire connections. Ronald Binge, the hugely successful Derby-born composer and arranger for the world-famous Mantovani orchestra, was rewarded with his own radio show on the BBC Light Programme. Binge's own composition, *String Song* provided the theme.

In the world of science, Chesterfield-born Robert Robinson, son of William Bradbury Robinson, founder of the successful Robinson's Healthcare company, and himself recipient of the 1947 Nobel Prize for Chemistry, announced his retirement. However, Robinson had no intention of staying idle: he was appointed an Honorary Fellow of Magdalen College, and director of the Shell Chemical Company.

International attention, meanwhile, was focused on the complex political nature of post-war Europe and beyond. With Germany now seemingly permanently divided into capitalist and communist halves, the Cold War between members of NATO and those of the Soviet-inspired Warsaw Pact became the over-riding concern of governments the world over.

For the average Briton, these issues seemed largely remote. For one Derbyshire native, however, such concerns had a more immediate and personal nature: he was to become an important cog in the machinery to fight the "Red Threat". Peter Wright was born in Chesterfield in 1916, the son of a Marconi engineer. He had served with the Admiralty's Research Laboratory during the Second World War and had also acted as an unpaid advisor to MI5. In 1954 he had been called in to help the CIA deal with bugging devices installed in the American embassy in Moscow. Now, in 1955, he was to join MI5's A2 branch as Principal Scientist.

In his controversial autobiography *Spycatcher*, Wright would later recall the words of one of his bosses, when he asked about MI5's legal status, "It hasn't got one. The Security Service cannot have the normal status of a Whitehall department because its work very often involves transgressing propriety or the law."

Derbyshire-born Wright also recalled that the organisation worked on the basis of the unofficial the 11th commandment: "Thou shalt not get caught."

Wright's work with the security services included many surveillance operations, including ENGULF, in which listening devices were used to monitor the sound of a mechanical cipher machine to establish which codes were being used; STOCKADE, which read the electro-magnetic echoes of the cipher at the French embassy; and RAFTER, which detected the frequencies of radio receivers and was used against the Soviets.

The mid-1950s was indeed a time of enormous political intrigue and instability, but if one son of the county was fully enmeshed in this James Bond world, for the people of Derbyshire generally there was comfort in a time of peace and prosperity.

1956

Derby Playhouse destroyed by fire

BRITAIN'S weakening influence in the Middle East, a sudden influx of foreign refugees causing resentment in Derbyshire, the problems of the homeless, and plans for the expansion of the nuclear power industry: sounds familiar? They were all issues capturing headlines in the mid-1950s.

More mundane matters also made big news in the *Derby Evening Telegraph*. In 1956. On 28 March, the front page of the newspaper featured a picture of actress Ann Kennedy as she examined the charred remains of her professional home – the Derby Playhouse.

In the early hours of that morning fire had swept through the theatre, leaving the venue all but devastated. PC Albert Smith, who had first noticed smoke filling Sacheverel Street, had raised the alarm. As flames "shot through the roof" of the former Baptist Sunday School building, residents of neighbouring properties were hastily evacuated.

Derby Playhouse had moved to the site in 1952, from its first home in a former schoolroom on Becket Street. The Playhouse,

In March 1956, Derby Playhouse in Sacheverel Street was gutted by fire. This picture shows all that was left of the auditorium.

The fire station that stood in Bold Lane, pictured here in the mid-1950s.

and its predecessor, the Derby Little Theatre, had become well known for its popular and acclaimed weekly rep.

With the stage, stalls and circle entirely burnt out and the roof collapsed, plans were immediately under way for repairs, although it was clear that it would be many months before any further performances could be staged. The *Telegraph* noted, with irony, that that week's performance was named *The Wick and the Wax*, and the following week's *High Temperature*.

Mixed reception for commercial television

WHILE theatre was still very popular with Derbyshire audiences, it was the new medium of television that really captured the average Derbeian's attention. From February, local viewers become the first outside of London to receive the new commercial television station, ITV.

Midlands Television, as it was known locally, was based in Birmingham and was broadcast on Channel 8. To view the new programmes an up-to-date set, or at least one which had been adapted, was required.

Mr W. E. Webb, chairman of the Derby Centre of the Radio and Television Retailers' Association, told the *Telegraph*: "Most people seem to have left conversion late ... In the last fortnight we have had quite a rush, and we now have a waiting list. All my own staff have been working every night during this period. From our experience in Derby most viewers will definitely need a new aerial to receive ITV ... using the proper aerial, you get an ITV picture three times as good as that received with a Band I aerial."

Across the county, the clarity and strength of the signal varied considerably. In Ripley it proved very strong, but in the valley around Matlock it was very disappointing. In Derby the signal was clear and bright, and one Derby television dealer took great delight in pronouncing: "Reception was absolutely astounding. We got a marvellous picture, every bit as good, if not better, than BBC."

The first night's viewing began with an official opening ceremony, before an evening of news and sport, followed by a variety show featuring established stars like singer Barbara Lyon – the daughter of radio veterans Ben Lyon and Bebe Daniels; actor Tyrone Power; children's entertainer "Mr Pastry" (Richard Hearne); and comedian Bob Monkhouse. Following this was an episode of *I Love Lucy*, starring Lucille Ball and Desi Arnaz.

Most of the fortunate local households, among the one million viewers across the region, declared the channel was well worth the investment in new equipment.

During the week, programming was provided by Associated Television Ltd (ATV) and at weekends by Associated British Cinemas (ABC). From May 1956, a nightly *Midlands News* was introduced.

However, for many people the cost of a television set was quite out of reach. The *Evening Telegraph* carried an advertisement for the latest Sobell Seventeen, a 17in set with a "handsome walnut veneered cabinet". It was on sale for 69 guineas – almost £73. That was a staggering amount considering that Derby jewellers Joseph Golding were advertising an engagement ring at £7 10s (£7.50) and a 22ct gold wedding ring at £3 5s 0d (£3.25).

Many people chose not to invest because they had heard scare stories that watching television was dangerous. The county ophthalmologist, however, tried to put their minds at rest.

Several Derbyshire clinics had been seeing increased numbers of children suffering from nasty headaches after watching television, which had alarmed parents. It was pointed out, however, that this was caused by sitting too close to the set and could be remedied by sitting a minimum of 6ft away with the set positioned straight ahead. The headaches would soon melt away with no lasting damage. Television, the *Telegraph* reassured readers, was "not injurious to children's eyes".

Refugees from Hungary

LUXURIES like televisions were far from the minds of the many Hungarian refugees who had sought safety here after the Soviet military had smashed their uprising. Donington Hall, just over the border in Leicestershire, but only a few miles from Derby, had been converted into a reception centre for the refugees.

Once the home of the Earl of Moira, and later the property of the Gillies Shields family, the hall had been converted for use as a prisoner-of-war camp during the First World War. In 1915, a German pilot, Gunther Pluschow, had made one of the few successful escape attempts from a British-run POW camp. Forty-one years later, ITV television news showed staff and volunteers cleaning and repairing the building in preparation for its temporary residents.

Most Britons were very welcoming to the initial influx of 11,000 refugees. There was great sympathy for their situation and their cause and, according to some commentators, considerable guilt at the inaction of the British Government on their behalf.

A letter to the *Telegraph* from the Gillies Shields, and Joyce Pearce of Donington Hall, thanked all those who were assisting them – providing clothing, books and toys for the children.

It promised that, once the immediate crisis was over, it was their intention to turn Donington Hall into "a home and school for children of all nationalities who now live without hope in the displaced persons camps in Germany, their parents were our allies, their sufferings caused through loyalty to our cause."

Other local residents, however, considered these newcomers were more a problem. One such critic, writing under the pseudonym "Chaddesden", objected strongly to Shardlow Rural District County's decision to offer a council house rent-free to a Hungarian family for six months.

"No matter how many people of other nationalities seek refuge in this country, they always thrive at the expense of our own people. Vast sums of money are collected, help given to buy houses and disused buildings turned into first-class homes for them – first class that is, in comparison to the homes of thousands of our own countrymen", the writer complained. "What a welcome change it would make to hear of such large sums of money and houses being given to our own old age pensioners and needy couples with family trying to start a home going."

This correspondent was clearly not the first to complain. Another writer, who signed themselves "Live and Let Live", wrote to express astonishment at "a contribution from "Alvastonite" a few days earlier. "I cannot think how a person could be so selfish as to begrudge the poor people a house. I would welcome any foreigner into my home as I have never met such kind, clean and unselfish people ... Just think yourself lucky you have a home and a country."

Derby Town Council, meanwhile, was trying to lessen some of its own responsibilities in relation to the burden of caring for the local homeless. Following a recommendation from its Welfare Committee, the council planned to petition that the provision and maintenance of what the *Telegraph* called "hobo reception centres" be transferred to the National Assistance Board.

The newspaper reported that, during October alone, some 60 men each night were using the centre, and that it had taken 1,127 admissions, with only 22 placed in employment.

Reasons for optimism

AS the year drew to a close, the *Evening Telegraph* assessed the state of local industry. Although it was conceded that "international uncertainties and their effect on Britain's economy make it difficult to look into Derby's industrial future", the paper was able to point out several reasons for optimism.

Of particular note was the likelihood of Derby's role in the somewhat controversial expansion of Britain's nuclear power "which in the next decade are likely to underpin Britain's economy".

International Combustion was named as one of three members of the British Atomic Group, which had been formed to construct several nuclear power stations. Another member was Crompton Parkinson, whose Derby Cables were expected to assist in construction.

Aiton & Co had already installed important pipework at Calder Hall "A" Nuclear Power Station in Cumberland. And Rolls-Royce was researching into the various applications of nuclear energy. At the behest of their chairman, Lord Hives, a small research team had been created to investigate nuclear power as a possible source of power for engines, in particular in ships, aircraft and submarines. They were working from their Advanced Research Department at the Old Hall on Burton Road in Littleover, where a laboratory and rig shop had been built.

The firm's aero engine division was also prospering, having received a great many international orders for its engines. Rolls-

Royce products were now operating in 543 countries from the Arctic Circle to New Zealand.

Royal Crown Derby, meanwhile, had been asked to create a 750-piece banqueting service for the Royal York Hotel in Toronto – the largest and most distinguished hotel in Canada. If the international situation was still cause for concern, the people of Derbyshire, at least it seemed, could look forward to a more settled year ahead.

1957

Railway works wrecked by fire

A MASSIVE fire at one of the county's most important and world-acclaimed industrial concerns, a preoccupation with the drudgery of housework, and a determination to give up the unhealthy habit of smoking – they were all issues that concerned the people of Derbyshire in 1957.

On the morning of 10 September, the *Evening Telegraph* reported in dramatic style: "Night Blaze Wrecks Derby Rail Shop Bays".

The rail shop in question was the Carriage and Wagon works in Litchurch, beside the Midland Station. One of the country's most important railway manufactories, it had been established by the Midland Railway and had suffered severe damage during the First World War, in the Zeppelin raid of February 1916.

The effects of the 1957 fire could be seen from a great distance. The *Evening Telegraph* reported: "At the height of the blaze, which cast a glow in the sky visible for miles, flames leaped 50 feet into the air and threatened to engulf two other bays."

Only the quick thinking of several employees had prevented further catastrophe: "Railway personnel succeeded in pulling clear some of the carriages undergoing repair in the affected bays – but others were quickly reduced to blackened, twisted steel frameworks, silhouetted against blazing wooden beams and smouldering debris."

Derby's deputy chief fire officer, Mr S. B. Jowett, who had taken charge of the fire fight, reported that, even though some 20 jets were aimed at the blaze as well as two turntable ladders and 15 pumps being called into action, it had proved difficult to prevent the fire spreading further, because the flames were being fanned by a stiff breeze. Insufficient water supplies had also caused the fire brigade difficulties, and hoses had to be stretched a quarter of a mile away to mains hydrants in London Road, and to a pond at Ascot Drive.

Fortunately, no one was hurt in the fire that, initial evidence suggested, had been accidental. Early concerns that the damage might cause significant loss of business, and affect local jobs, were soon put at ease. "Men's jobs safe," the *Evening Telegraph* reassured workers and their families.

Earthquake!

ON the afternoon of 11 February 1957, an earthquake measuring 5.3 on the Richter scale struck Derby. Felt right across central England, it was the largest UK post-war earthquake until 1984. It was one of the most destructive shakes Britain has ever seen. There was much damage to masonary and roofs and it was felt as far away as Hartlepool, Pwllheli in Wales, Norwich and Topsham, near Exeter. Derby was also the epicentre of the first UK earthquake to be recorded instrumentally, in March 1903

Chatsworth's treasures threatened

THE loss of many of Derbyshire's rural treasures to the museums and establishments of London would eventually have far-reaching effects on the way the nation viewed its stately homes, art treasures and its gentry.

The *Derby Evening Telegraph* of 6 September 1957 revealed that the 11th Duke of Devonshire had been forced to hand over to the Treasury some of his family's estates and chattels in order to settle the death duties left by the 10th Duke.

Ironically, this system of death duties – in which tax was imposed upon all the land and personal property of a deceased person, rather than on the amount of property inherited by their beneficiaries – had been introduced by a Derby MP, the Liberal Chancellor of the Exchequer, Sir William Harcourt, in 1894.

Since a large estate taxed as one entity would see more tax at the higher rates than that imposed on several smaller inheritances, the law had proved highly unpopular, particularly with the wealthy and aristocratic, many of whom who saw it as a personal attack on their class. Many more also realised that, within a few generations, their entire estates might be lost, having been carved up, piece by piece, to pay off various death duties.

The 9th Duke of Devonshire had been the first of his line to have to pay death duties, and these had amounted to more than half a million pounds. Coupled with significant debts left over from the failure of the 7th Duke's business ventures, the family had already been forced to sell many precious possessions to settle their bills. In 1912 many books, including rare first editions of Shakespeare, had been sold to a library in California; and in 1920, Devonshire House and its lands in Piccadilly had also been sold.

The 10th Duke's sudden death seven years earlier, at the age of 55, had left huge debts- at the maximum rate of 80 per cent tax – to be paid before his heirs could inherit, and careful negotiations with the Treasury had established a plan by which this could be settled.

As the *Evening Telegraph* revealed, this meant the removal of seven art treasures, worth an estimated £1 million, to the British Museum in London. Works by Rembrandt, Van Dyck, Holbein and Memlinc had been carefully removed from the house, under total secrecy, even while visitors toured other parts of the estate.

Indeed, so secret was the activity that the British Museum had already been displaying several items, including the head of Apollo cast in bronze, dating from around 485 BC, the *Book of Truth of Claude Lorrain*, and the Van Dyck sketch book, even before the *Evening Telegraph* could reveal the move. Other items were taken to the National Gallery and the National Portrait Gallery.

In addition, it was revealed, the Treasury was to receive the lovely Hardwick Hall, the personal creation of Bess of Hardwick – at one time the richest woman in England after her queen, Elizabeth I. The Hall itself and its contents, farms and estates would then be passed on to the National Trust.

Predictably, local reaction was strong. There was horror that such local treasures could be spirited away from Derbyshire and displayed in London. A meeting of 13 local authorities was held in Matlock, where calls were made for the treasures to be retained in the north of England at least.

Royal visit

IN March 1957, the Queen and Prince Phillip arrived at Derby Midland station. The Queen, accompanied by the Mayor of

Troops line up in Derby Market Place in March 1957, ready to be inspected by the Queen.

Derby, Councillor J. H. Christmas, visited the Leylands Cottage Homes, off Broadway, in Derby, inspected a guard of honour in Derby Market Place and went to Burton, Tutbury and Repton, while Prince Phillip went to the the Leicestershire and Derbyshire Yeomanry depot on Siddals Road, where he chatted to wives and children of servicemen and inspected veterans.

Good year for sport and entertainment

FOR local sports fans, 1957 proved a more satisfying year. At Easter, Derby County achieved promotion to the Second Division, after two seasons in the Third Division North, and Derbyshire's cricketers fared well against the West Indians. In June, they bowled out the tourists, whose team included the great Clyde Walcott, Frank Worrall and Sonny Ramadhin, for just 115 runs at Chesterfield. There was to be no famous victory, however – the West Indians recovered to win by 173 runs.

The success of local people in the entertainment industry continued unabated. Derbyshire-born John Dexter joined the Royal Court Theatre as a director. He had been raised in Leyland Street, Derby, the son of a lorry driver, and had been educated at Gerard Street School, although he was somewhat sensitive about his roots.

His early life had given little indication of his talents. Dexter was a poor scholar and left school at 14 to work in a factory. After National Service, however, he turned to acting and found work in repertory in Derby, and with the BBC, playing a village policeman in a new radio drama serial, *The Archers*. In the mid-1950s, he had joined the staff of the Central School of Speech and Drama in London before taking on his new role. Although Dexter had little experience, his enthusiasm and imagination for this new direction was encouraging, and he was thought by many to the potential to become one of the greatest talents the country had produced.

Darby and Joan

AT the turn of the year, the *Evening Telegraph*'s Darby and Joan column, which was aimed at its older readership, asked local people to reveal their New Year resolutions. There seemed to be a common theme. Viscountess Scarsdale, of Kedleston Hall declared: "I could give up smoking, but I'd never keep it up." Mrs J. R. Ratcliffe, Derby town councillor and prospective Conservative candidate as MP for Belper, was more positive: "I shall try to smoke less and try to do a little less grumbling."

But Jack Longland, director of education for the county, was already regretting some of his resolutions, even though the New Year was yet to arrive. "I did say way back in November that I would give up smoking. Already I've learned that one shouldn't make rash promises so far in advance, but we shall see."

Darby and Joan had suggestions for local housewives. The New Year sales at Thurman and Malin in St Peter's Street featured, according to their advertisement running beside the column, "many articles at half price or less ... Bargains in all departments". At another sale, at John Plant of Irongate, many brands of shoes would be "reduced by approximately 6s 8d".

But Darby and Joan cautioned readers: "Take an honest fashion-eye view of yourself."

The column also offered housekeeping advice: "See whether all your journeys back and forth through the house are really necessary... Sort the most used articles closer together ... buy aprons with larger pockets so that you can carry dusters ... stop reaching and stretching, or carrying heavy chairs ... Invest in a lightweight stool with steps combined."

Doubtless it was advice of which fellow contributor, Ella Lewis Cox, would have approved. In a feature that would certainly provoke a deluge of angry readers' letters in the 21st century, Ms Cox pointed a controversial finger at lazy housewives. Her article, entitled "Queen of Leisure" claimed that no modern housewife should be tired at the end of the day. If they were, "then they have frittered away the day in order to fill it out with something to do... I believe that thousands of women are deliberately, if unconsciously, spoiling their enjoyment of life by their silly belief that housewifery is serfdom and marriage a sentence of hard labour".

In what was doubtless intended as a compliment to the abilities of women everywhere, Ms Cox declared: "A woman's capacity for work is enormous. This summer... I visited a farm [in France] where the wife ran the great old house, cooked on a wood fire, kept 300 head of poultry, brought up four children and was still able to take a two-hour siesta at midday and preside over a splendid evening meal as if she were a visitor. All she had to help her was a little maidservant." The fact that all this work was apparently divided between two women was, presumably, not lost on Ms Cox's readers.

But Ms Cox's claims were not without scientific backup. "With the help of a time and motion study engineer, I have worked out the actual time involved in routine jobs on a normal day in a modern semi-detached house of three bedrooms and two reception rooms."

Between 8.35 am and 10.45 am, Ms Cox estimated the housewife should have completed the following tasks: preparing breakfast for her husband and son and eating her own; clearing away the pots; handwashing some clothing; cleaning the kitchen; tidying, vacuuming and dusting the living room; cleaning the hall and stairs; making the beds; cleaning the bedrooms and spare room; and cleaning the bathroom, landing and toilet.

The housewife that Ms Cox had embroiled in her time and motion study was clearly unhappy with the conditions. She had wanted to enjoy a third cup of tea, read the newspaper, listen to a favourite song on *Housewives Choice*, natter to a neighbour while hanging out the washing, and so on. Ms Cox, it seemed, had pointed out to her that, rather than complain, she should be grateful that she was not at work in a factory, as many of her "sisters" were – their work would not be over by mid-morning. Certainly it was true that the introduction of labour-saving devices had made the work of the average British housewife much less back-breaking, but it would be some years before she might look forward to spending most of her life outside of the home and its responsibilities.

1958

More Derby drunks than ever before

AT the beginning of 1958 the *Evening Telegraph* revealed that convictions for drunkenness, which were the highest since the war, were causing concern among many Derby folk. With no less than 321 convictions in 1957 alone, a sharp increase of 93 on the previous year, there were fears of a trend that might be difficult to turn around.

Derby's Chief Constable, Mr E. V. Staines, said that there was no need for alarm, since 47.35 per cent of those convicted were not residents of the county. He was concerned, however, at assaults on police officers, which numbered seven in the year, and which were becoming ever more common.

"Our officers are only doing their duty and it is un-British of the public to take advantage of policemen who are, after all, only doing their job and who are not permitted to retaliate."

Mr Staines felt the licensees themselves were greatly to blame, since they flagrantly disregarded warnings not to serve alcohol to those already intoxicated. There had been many prosecutions against licensees, most of which had been in relation to allowing drinking outside of licensing hours.

Perhaps more worryingly Mr Staines noted with "grave concern" the increasing number of people arrested for driving a motor vehicle while under the influence of drink.

Twisted metal and burnt-out carriages pictured after the 1958 fire at the Carriage and Wagon Works.

Another railway works fire

RECOVERY from the huge fire at Derby's Carriage and Wagon works in the autumn of 1957 had taken considerable effort and time. So it was with absolute horror that the *Telegraph* reported a second fire in less than a year at one of Derby's major employers.

On the evening of 8 September 1958, almost a year to the day after the previous fire, 19 year-old Brian Walker, an employee of the Carriage and Wagon Works, was playing bowls near his workplace.

He told the *Evening Telegraph* his story: "I caught sight of what must have been the fire about 7.55pm. There was just a little wisp of dark smoke coming up and I didn't take any notice of it. About five or ten minutes later I happened to look again in the same direction and the top of the shed was all aglow. There were no flames."

With Brian was Gary Morton, one of the Carriage and Wagon Works' own firemen, who raced off to alert his colleagues.

Witnesses reported several small explosions and a much larger one about an hour later. Many Derbeians, astonished that another huge fire could again strike the same business, gathered on the Long Bridge over the Derwent, to watch the "searing wall of fire". Eventually the police were forced to clear spectators from the area, in case flying debris landed there. By 10.30pm fire fighters declared the blaze under control, although it would be more than an hour before it was extinguished entirely.

Again the damage was severe and one of the buildings entirely rebuilt after the last blaze lay, once more, in ashes. Indeed, the devastation was even greater than before and, as *Evening Telegraph* photographs showed, much of the complex was reduced to a tangle of charred and mangled girders.

Derby's most famous vegetarian

IN August, the *Evening Telegraph* interviewed 89-year-old Derbyshire resident Frank Walters – a vegetarian since 1893. Despite a "diet that would make every lover of a succulent steak wince", Mr Walters was happy to tell readers that he continued to enjoy an active and fulfilled life. For many years, Mr Walters had been the postmaster at Pentrich and a typical day's food might be two apples and a cup of tea for breakfast, lightly boiled carrots and potatoes for dinner and for tea lettuce, brown bread and butter, a cup of tea and a little jam.

While many *Evening Telegraph*'s readers, even those living in more health-conscious times, might balk at so limited a diet, Mr Walters proudly told readers that he was still fit enough to keep up a large garden and until very recent times, had regularly walked the 12 miles from his home into Derby. He put his health and longevity entirely down to his diet, his lifetime of abstention from alcohol and his refusal to smoke tobacco. A vehement opponent of nuclear weapons, Mr Walters told *the Evening Telegraph* that he felt it was also immoral to kill animals for food.

Appropriately Mr Walters, who was fluent in the international language of Esperanto, had named his neat blue and white Pentrich cottage "La Sana Vivo" – Esperanto for the healthy life.

Local folk honoured

IF other sons and daughters of the county were not so preoccupied, they were certainly making their mark on the national and international scene. Chesterfield-born-and-educated Nobel Laureate Robert Robinson, son of William Bradbury Robinson, founder of Robinsons of Chesterfield, was made president of the Society for the Chemical Industry.

Baroness Ravensdale, daughter of George Nathaniel Curzon, 1st Marquis Curzon of Kedleston, was made one of the first four female life peers. Although she was, by birth, a socialite and boasted Noel Coward and Ivor Novello among her friends, like her father the former Foreign Secretary and Viceroy of India, the Baroness was extremely politically aware and an active supporter of many charities, particularly those that assisted young people.

Chesterfield-born MP Barbara Castle became chairman of the Labour Party. Known affectionately as the Red Queen, Mrs Castle had already served in a succession of junior roles in several Labour governments since becoming an MP in 1945.

Elsewhere, a young Ilkeston-born actor, William Roache, secured his first professional role in the film *Behind the Mask* – a medical drama starring Michael Redgrave, Tony Brittain and a young Vanessa Redgrave.

Soggy Derbyshire, recovering Rams ... and foul play at the dog track?

THE sporting year in Derbyshire was severely affected by the inclement weather. Most notably during the wet and cold summer Derbyshire CCC had only two of their 15 home games uninterrupted by the weather. In total 113 hours and 5 minutes of Derbyshire's play were lost to the rain, with the county club affected on 43 of 90 possible days' play. It seemed each day's rain would begin just as supporters prepared to leave for the ground. As a result, the club reported losses of £10,735 on the season. Fortunately, the Supporters' Club had insured a number of home matches against rain interruption and were able to present the club with £1,318 to offset some of the losses.

The bad weather did little to dent the enthusiasm of the boys of Bemrose Grammar School whose headmaster, Dr Eric Bennett, allowed them to take an afternoon off from school to watch Derbyshire entertain the New Zealand touring side at the County Ground in June.

For Derby County, 1958 was a mixed year. By November, the Rams had fallen to 17th in the old Second Division and relegation talk was rife in the town. Eventually, an amazing turnaround of fortune would see them finish the 1958-59 season in seventh place. Rams fans would have to wait for 1959 to realise that achievement, but the turning point came on 20 November 1958, with a 3-2 home win over Liverpool.

Regulars at Derby's greyhound track on Vernon Street were shocked to learn of the sudden deaths of three greyhounds at the

Derby Greyhound Stadium at the end of Vernon Street, on the site of the former county prison, the façade of which survives into the 21st century.

track. Although the deaths of Chip Off The Old Block, Clean Sand and Queen Colburn appeared to be due to "heart failure", officials took the decision to suspend racing until post mortem results from the Canine Research Centre of the Animal Health Trust could be completed.

The track's representative, Mr G. W. Turnpenney, said that even though there was no evidence of foul play, he felt it "only fair to the private owners whose dogs race here". It was eventually concluded that each of the dogs had died due to accidental exposure to the warfarin poison set down to eradicate rats and mice from the stadium.

New market for Allenton

IN December, the *Evening Telegraph* revealed the Town Council's plans for a new open market for Allenton. "Plans are well advanced," noted the paper. The market was to comprise 90 stalls where traders would do business under brightly coloured "tilts" or canvas awnings in an atmosphere "strongly reminiscent of the old trading days in Derby Market Place".

Rather than create a state-of-the-art market, the council had decided to build a "market resembling those which Derby knew in its past", said Alderman C. F. Bowman, chairman of the council's Markets Committee.

An area of land along Osmaston Road, near the Mitre Hotel – formerly allotments – had already been set aside for the construction of the market. The stalls would be placed on a concrete base and be provided with a car park and plenty of space for the market to expand. Alderman Bowman hoped that, since the council merely had to approve the plans, work would begin early in 1959 and that by spring "everything will be ready for a glorious opening".

He continued: "We are convinced that, with the goodwill of traders and people in the district, we shall make a huge success of the new market."

With plans well under way for a new town abattoir and a proposal to build a new cattle market on the Little Meadow off Nottingham Road under consideration, Alderman Bowman felt that the new market would be "another jewel in our crown".

1959

Derby MP awarded Nobel Peace Prize

WHEN Derbyshire sweltered in record-breaking temperatures during the summer of 1959, no one had heard the expression "global warming". Other news items, however, made familiar headlines – UFOs, racial prejudice, a tragic industrial accident to name but three. Comprehensive education also seemed a step nearer; and a familiar face of Derby was about to change.

Derby MP Philip Noel-Baker was awarded the Nobel Peace Prize.

In 1959, one of Derby's best-loved adopted sons, Philip Noel-Baker – one of the town's MPs for more than 20 years – was awarded the Nobel Peace Prize for a lifetime's work promoting peace and disarmament, work during the Russian Famine in the late 1920s and with refugees during World War Two.

It was another shining achievement for a remarkable man who had represented Britain at three Olympic Games, winning a silver medal in the 1,500 metres at Antwerp in 1920, and had been decorated for bravery during the First World War, when the Quaker and pacifist had served as an ambulance driver. On receiving the honour Noel-Baker said: "War is a damnable, filthy thing and has destroyed civilisation after civilisation – that is the essence of my belief." In its Picture

Edition the *Evening Telegraph* produced a special feature on the ceremony and television viewers were also able to see the MP receive the honour at the Great Hall of Oslo University in the first Nobel ceremony televised across Europe.

Racial prejudice

IN May, the *Evening Telegraph* published a feature by one of its regular columnists "Albert Street" asking: "Has Derby a Colour Bar?" As new immigrants had begun arriving from the Commonwealth, there had been much talk of non-white school leavers finding it difficult to obtain suitable work in the town because employers were selecting white workers ahead of them, regardless of qualification or ability. As the columnist pointed out, it would be hard to prove this was the case since: "No firm will admit publicly … that the colour of an apprentice's skin could affect his chances of securing an apprenticeship".

He also suggested that fear of an unfavourable reaction from existing workers might put employers off taking on immigrant workers. The previous year, factory workers at Milford had gone on strike when a Punjabi was given work there. The strikers had claimed that the management had agreed not to take on "coloured" workers when white workers were available. Albert Street was horrified to relate that, although the two sides had eventually reached an agreement, this had occurred only after the Punjabi had been dismissed.

The columnist believed the "traditional insularity of the British" and a general mistrust and dislike of anything visibly non-British was to blame. "It may be fair to argue that when in Britain you should do as the British do, although heaven knows why you should, provided you are not breaking any laws."

Despite his concerns Albert Street was convinced that there was very little disharmony in the town. "Derby strikes me as an admirable example to many towns in the way that it accepts our guests from other lands."

Traffic is building up in Irongate in 1959.

Undoubtedly differences in the way that people of different colours and cultures were treated and viewed existed right across Britain, whether this was intentional or not. Doubtless in part because non-white immigration was still very new to the town, even the *Evening Telegraph* took pains to point out that, during a drugs raid on a house party in Leacroft Road in September: "93 of the people at party [were] coloured."

Newspaper workers' strike

In late June, a national printing dispute erupted. While national newspapers were unaffected, work at all regional newspapers, including the *Evening Telegraph,* and at printing works like Bemrose's in Litchurch, was brought to a halt. Throughout the six-week strike, non-union workers at the *Evening Telegraph* produced a small "emergency bulletin" for its readers. Initially, this took the form of a four-page typewritten publication, but later evolved into a small printed edition. For striking workers times were hard – strike pay was minimal – but eventually the print and paper workers became the first manual workers to secure a 40-hour working week.

A sweltering summer – but Derbeians still fly away

1959 would prove one of the warmest years in living memory. Although January was very cold, it was the sunniest on record and every other month produced higher than average temperatures. There was a long, hot, dry summer which lasted from early May to mid-October. Even with windows wide open, locals found restful sleep a rare commodity, and working in the factories, mills and foundries in particular became highly unpleasant. For children, of course, the long summer meant plenty of opportunities to enjoy the county's parks and to play in the streets.

In case the fine English weather had not satisfied Derbyshire folk, international air travel was now on offer. Under the tagline, "Fly Derby and meet the sun!" Derby Airways – the forerunner of BMI – advertised flights to Dublin, Guernsey, Jersey and the more exotic climes of Ostend, Luxembourg and Corsica. The airline operated out of Derby Airport at Burnaston, which had been opened in 1937 and for much of the Second World War had served as a flight-training centre for the RAF.

Another advertisement, this time for Derby travel agents, Briggs and Hill, in St Peter's Street, offered a "wonderful holiday in Jersey" with return flights from Derby, full board hotel accommodation, "wonderful full-day and half-day excursions", the services of a holiday rep, free baggage insurance and a "guarantee of a full refund in case of illness". All of this cost just £19 5s. Unfortunately, the advertisement neglected to mention the length of the holiday.

Stay at home and spend

IF Derbeians preferred to spend their hard-earned wages on something more tangible in 1959, there were plenty of advertisements from local businesses to investigate. Telefusion of London Road offered "unbeatable all-in rental terms" for a range of televisions, including the new Murphy 17-inch tabletop set.

Alex Owen Ltd on London Road was promoting a new Jackson refrigerator for 35 guineas. Alternatively, the same appliance could be bought on hire-purchase with a deposit of £7 10s followed by 104 weekly payments of 6s 2d. The attraction of immediately acquiring a gleaming new fridge that could, for an additional charge, be supplied with legs, might well have encouraged many a house-proud Derbeian to part with an extra ten per cent.

Other advertisements catered to mothers keen to give their sons "pride in their appearance", like that placed by Strand Boys' Clothiers & Outfitters who could supply suits, sports coats, rainwear, blazers, pullovers and even jeans. "Your boys," the advertisement reminded mothers, "deserve a good and reasonably priced outfit."

Perhaps the fashion-conscious Derby lady might have been tempted by the Derby Co-operative Society's promotion of Ballerina fully-fashioned nylon stockings. The "bewitching Ballerina nylons" were "the finest stockings money can buy" and featured a special "ladder stop" at top and bottom for longer-lasting wear.

For the wealthier Derbeian, a number of shoe shops in the county could provide "Gimpy – walking leisure, fashion pleasure" women's shoes. There was the Kitten for "party time"; or the Walkabout for the "Lady of Leisure", both of which could be purchased for 39s 11d. Alternatively, for another 10 shillings the customer could choose the Court for "that special occasion". Douglas Worth of the Wardwick offered fashion furs that could be offered in part exchange for "old furs".

A UFO ... and some comprehensive eductaion

IN June, the *Evening Telegraph* reported a "strange object, which appeared to be hanging motionless in the sky above the Derby area". One of the first to spot the UFO was Alfred Green of Mickleover, a special constable, and the following morning dozens of calls were placed by curious, and somewhat concerned, Derbeians. However, any fears of alien invasion, or of Soviet spies over the Rolls-Royce works, were soon soothed. A spokesman from the RAF identified the object as a large meteorological balloon.

Fortunately, more earthbound concerns tended to dominate the year. A petition, organised by Mr K. Langstaff of Duffield, was sent to the Minister of Education, requesting a public enquiry into plans by Derbyshire Education Committee to introduce comprehensive education to the county's schools. Certainly there was increasing dissatisfaction across the country at the standard of secondary modern schools, and a number of education authorities had already introduced the system to replace the threefold grammar school-technical-secondary modern status quo. The first comprehensive school had been at Holyhead in Anglesey and the new system had been introduced to great acclaim in Coventry, Sheffield, West Riding and in Leicestershire. But Mr Langstaff remained cautious. "Although it may work in other counties, we do not know that it will work in Derbyshire."

A factory tragedy

AFTER the Christmas holiday, workers at Garford-Lilley & Bros mill on Agard Street returned to work to find a strong smell of gas throughout the building. The *Evening Telegraph* reported that, far from immediately evacuating the property, work was able to continue after ventilation and tests. As Gas Board officials searched for the source of the leak, and fireman stood by hoses at the ready, in case of fire, work continued, much to the dissatisfaction of employees, many of whom were feeling ill from the effects of the fumes.

Mr W. K. Astbury, works manager, told the *Evening Telegraph*: "If it gets no worse, we shall carry on working, but if it does get worse we shall have to close down the factory." With more and more women feeling ill, the mill was eventually evacuated and, after a 12-hour search, the leak was traced to an underground gas pipe outside the factory.

For workers at another Derbyshire factory, December took a more tragic turn. On 2 December, four men were killed when part of Belper's historic North Mill, then occupied by the English Sewing Cotton Company Ltd, collapsed. The accident happened as routine demolition work on the mill's Round Building took place. Many of the 20 or so who escaped serious injury reported a rumble like thunder as the entire three-storey building collapsed. The first victim – Alfred Ritson – was discovered soon after the collapse, but the others – John Clarke, Arthur Freeman and Sam Gotheridge – remained trapped, and it was several hours before their bodies could be removed from the rubble. At the inquest, the coroner reported: "It was one of those things; there was no reason for it."

Derby's skyline begins to change

AS 1959 drew to a close, Derbeians looked forward to developments in the townscape. The first tower block of the new Derby and District College of Technology in Kedleston Road had opened, while the town's major department store, Ranby's, was preparing to move into new purpose-built premises. The store, which already had premises on Victoria Street, had acquired the 200-year-old Queen's Head pub next door. Publicans Mr & Mrs Fowler celebrated the last night of business at the end of December with a party for regulars who presented the couple with a parting gift.

While there was much sadness at the closing of one of Derby's oldest inns, this was matched by the anticipation of a much-enlarged Ranby's. The new store was expected to have two acres of sales room on the ground and first floors, while the third floor was to be devoted to a large restaurant, a hair salon and other

The Queen's Head pub in Victoria Street is sandwiched in the middle of the Ranby's store in this 1958 view.

services and would take three years to complete. There was much to look forward to as the 1960s dawned.

Derby in the Sixties

1960

A controversial new airport

THERE was both excitement and controversy at Derby Corporation's plans to reopen the former RAF airfield at Castle Donington. The council had previously expressed its intention to turn the airfield into a civilian airport as "a matter of policy" and wanted the first step to be to furnish the airport with a long hard runway.

However, the Castle Donington airfield stood within the county of Leicestershire, and John Chatterton, of Leicestershire County Council, told the *Evening Telegraph* that a planning application had been made by Derby Corporation, and that "it had always been Derby Borough's idea to take over the airfield on their own account and to develop it as an airport in place of the existing airport".

Certainly Derby Airport at Burnaston was becoming increasingly busy and an upgraded and enlarged alternative seemed increasingly necessary, but the council had previously mooted the idea that, rather than becoming a small civilian airport, Castle Donington might become a major airport for Derby and its neighbours Leicester and Nottingham.

For such a project to prosper, all three authorities would need to put in long-term investment to develop the wartime facilities to the required standards of the day. It was also widely assumed that, should such a scheme come into being, transatlantic flights would be making regular landings at the new airport.

There would be plenty of obstacles to overcome. Already many local residents had expressed their discomfort at a new airport, whether major or minor, with all its accompanying disruption and noise, opening up on their doorsteps.

New police building – but alarmingly low detection rates

MAJOR developments within Derby itself were also announced. The Derby Borough police force, then entirely independent from the Derbyshire County Constabulary, revealed plans to reorganise the force and to extend its headquarters in Full Street.

The Full Street police station, which had been built as part of Derby's Central Improvement Plan in the 1930s, was severely overcrowded with several offices spilling into corridors.

But, as the *Evening Telegraph's* Geoffrey Hammerton reported, new premises alone would not be enough to stem the seemingly ever-growing crime rate in the county. Figures, locally and nationally, indicated that crime was on an alarming rise, while detection rates were relatively low.

In the Borough, detection rates stood at just 65 per cent of the average of six crimes a day being reported, and the first six months of 1960 had revealed the highest reported crime rate on record. Reassuringly Chief Constable Noble announced he had instigated a number of measures with the "emphasis on preventing and detecting crime".

He had "stopped the 10pm curfew at the Central Police Station and instituted a 24-hour office". He also intended to organise a modern typing pool with "prefabricated" report forms to reduce the amount of paperwork done by his officers, leaving them "maximum time for positive policing".

Police motorcycles would be equipped with two-way radios and the CID department would be strengthened and expanded. The Borough would be divided into two divisions, each with their own modern police station. In addition: "There will be changes in foot and motor patrolling to increase the surprise element."

Bad news for Rolls-Royce

FOR Rolls-Royce, however, there was bad news in 1960s. The Government's planned Blue Streak ballistic missile project was cancelled. Since World War Two, Britain's nuclear deterrent had relied on atom bombs that had to be dropped from Vulcan aircraft.

However, if Britain wanted to possess a credible threat against Soviet attack, something that could be launched quickly from the UK towards the Soviet Union, it needed to own a ballistic missile system. The Government also realised the importance of producing a British-designed missile system, independent of the United States – thus ensuring that Britain could be seen as an independent nuclear power.

Rolls-Royce was chosen to manufacture the RZ2 engines that would power the missiles. The missiles themselves were to be built by De Havilland; Sperry Gyroscope produced the guidance system; and the Atomic Research Establishment at Aldermaston designed the warhead.

Ultimately Blue Streak was deemed impractical. The mix of kerosene and liquid oxygen that powered the missiles could not be mixed until needed. Fuelling would take at least 15 minutes, by which time any incoming Soviet missiles would have already reached their targets in Britain.

Blue Streak, it seemed, was hardly the deterrent everyone had been anticipating. In April the project was cancelled and a decision made to purchase American Skybolt missiles instead, although these too would eventually be abandoned in favour of the Polaris system.

TWO Derbyshire-born actors also shot to fame, this time in what would become the country's favourite, and longest-running, TV drama serial. Arthur Lowe was born in Hadfield, in the north of the county, in 1915 and became an actor after serving as a cavalry trooper during the Second World War. He had already enjoyed a busy theatrical career, and had earned small parts in films like *Kind Hearts and Coronets* (1949) and in radio's *Mrs Dale's Diary.*

In 1960, Lowe joined the cast of Granada Television's new series *Coronation Street* as Leonard Swindley. Alongside him was Ilkeston native William Roache. Like Lowe, Roache had pursued acting after a military career; in his case National Service with the Royal Welch Fusiliers took him to Germany, Jamaica, the Bahamas and the Persian Gulf. *Coronation Street* had initially been planned to run for only 13 weeks. Lowe remained with the show for seven years and Roache, more than 54 years later, is still starring as Ken Barlow.

DERBY-born billiards player, Herbert Beetham, won two major championships in 1960. Beetham was born in April 1909, at the Havelock Road factory house of White's Brothers, the family soft drinks manufacturing business that he ran for years. Although he had not taken up the sport seriously until the age of 19, he proved an instant success, first entering the English National Billiards Championships in 1932, and reaching the finals in 1946, 1952 and 1959.

In March 1960, Beetham took the title for the first time, beating Reg Wright of Leicestershire in final. "It was," he said later, "a wonderful moment in my life."

Six months later, Beetham topped even that achievement, becoming the first English world billiards champion since Walter

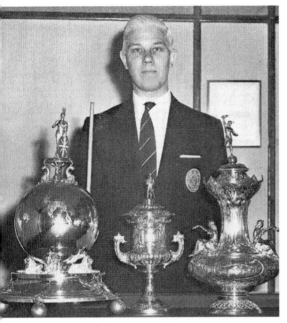

Derby's Herbert Beetham became world billiards champion in 1960.

Driffield's victory in Calcutta in 1952.

In the world final, Beetham met the Irish champion, W. J. Dennison, and although he was 100 points down at one stage, pulled back to win by 1,173 points to 845.

IN 1960, another sportsman was just embarking upon what would become a long and illustrious career for Derbyshire. Yet it was a career that almost never began. Young Staffordshire-born wicketkeeper, Bob Taylor, had been selected to make his debut for Derbyshire 2nd XI against Lancashire 2nds at St Helen's. He had been instructed to wait at Leek for Derbyshire's coach Denis Smith – himself one of the county's greatest players. Taylor waited and waited and was about to go home when Smith eventually arrived. Derbyshire – and England – would be grateful that Taylor had waited as long as he did.

In August 1960, the *Evening Telegraph* published a photograph of one of its former columnists. Gardener Percy Thrower was shown as he prepared the BBC's gardening section of the Radio Show at Earl's Court in London.

Although born in Buckinghamshire, Thrower had worked in the Royal Gardens in Windsor before joining Derby Corporation's Parks Department while in his 20s. From here he had moved to Shrewsbury, where the BBC's Godfrey Baseley, presenter of a radio programme called *Beyond the Back Door*, had spotted his talents. Thrower had become a noted expert in

The corner of East Street and the Morledge was still undeveloped in 1960.

his own right and was now "conductor of BBC TV's Gardening Club", as the *Telegraph* described him. He would later become television's first celebrity gardener.

In contrast, 1960 brought the sad news that Constance Spry, doyenne of middle-class housewives for her innovative and fashion-conscious floral arrangements, had died. Spry's wonderful arrangements had graced the homes of celebrities, socialites and royalty, and through her books she had reached out to the average housewife and showed them how to create elegant displays with wild flowers and even vegetables and fruit. Not bad for a girl born in Derby's Warner Street.

1961

Markets – "gaudy and gay"

THE modernisation of the traffic system, plans for a pedestrianised shopping area, a boom in bingo halls, and the near loss of a favourite county landmark – they all made headlines in the *Derby Evening Telegraph* in 1961.

As had been the case in most years since the end of the Second World War, new developments in town and county continued apace. The new Allenton market, in the making for the past three years, finally opened for business; it joined three town centre markets: the Victorian Market Hall, the market on Cockpit Hill, and, as the *Evening Telegraph* described it, the "gaudy, gay Morledge open market".

In fact, so impressive were Derby's markets that the *Telegraph* devoted a two-page feature to "The Lure of Derby Markets" and the "Glamour of the Stalls". But while an unnamed greengrocer in the Morledge was happy to say that, despite rising expenses, profit margins had remained the same, others warned that markets were in danger from big-name shops. "People are forsaking the markets for the large stores, that's the trend everywhere," cautioned one local haberdasher.

One of the problems seemed to be that markets were seen as the place for a great bargain. "They want something worth 15 bob for 10 bob – and you have to get it for them" claimed one trader.

The weather also presented differing fortunes for stallholders. A rainy day would usually see most people abandon the Morledge and Cockpit markets for the comfort of the indoor Market Hall.

"They can shop here in the dry and get everything they want," boasted one Market Hall stallholder. Another compared the Market Hall to the shopping centres of others towns: "This isn't really a market, it's a chain of shops."

The *Telegraph* noted that, at the Cockpit Hill market, "many of the traders are in the old tradition of market salesman, the type of person who must have been borne in mind when the expression 'gift of the gab' was coined".

Rather than using Corporation-supplied market stalls, traders here rented a pitch and erected their own tents and stalls,

Stalls on Cockpit Hill in the late 1960s.

or put up tables or simply laid their wares on the cobblestones. The banter of the markets, although "stale and corny" still provided enough entertainment to draw people over to watch, not least when Mad Harry was on top form.

Despite the claims of several stallholders that trade was "not was it used to be", the *Telegraph* reported that there was a waiting list for new stalls, that rarely was one given up and that, when it was, there would be at least 30 applications to take over. "Trade in Derby's markets is really pretty good," the paper reported.

The changing face of Derby

ELSEWHERE in Derby, work had begun on the new Bradshaw Way, between Traffic Street and Osmaston Road – the second phase of the Inner Ring Road scheme.

The council's "Operation Mole", to provide a two-and-a-half-mile-long tunnelled storm water culvert, was also well under way, while a range of state-of-the-art flats had been constructed on the former Little City at the top of Burton Road, just before the hill fell away into Babington Lane and Green Lane. The Little City's tight, narrow streets, built in Napoleonic times (evidenced by names like Cannon Street and Trafalgar Street) had effectively become a slum; the clean, modern flats regenerated the area considerably.

Derby's Civic Society was doing its bit to improve the more historic parts of the town, with a scheme to give Sadler Gate a facelift. However, the council also had plans for this ancient lane that had its origins in the Viking occupation of the town. An idea had been proposed by Councillor J.H. Christmas, a former mayor, to restrict vehicular access to Sadler Gate and this was causing something of an uproar, among traders at least.

George Dixon, proprietor of Dixons (Derby) Ltd, wrote a letter to the *Evening Telegraph* opposing the scheme, while praising the activities of the Civic Society whose work, according to Mr Dixon, would make Derby "very proud of this ancient street when it is finished".

However pedestrianisation, as Mr Dixon pointed out, would cause difficulties to local traders because most of the properties had no rear access.

A half-hour parking limit was already in place "and yet the street is always lined with cars, vans and lorries – adequate proof that the free access to our premises by road transport of all kinds, is vital to our very existence".

Mr Dixon called for the widening the George Yard, which ran virtually the length of Sadler Gate and could be adapted to provide rear access to at least one side of the street, and act as an alternate traffic route. "We would be very sorry indeed if our efforts only resulted in the singling out of Sadler Gate for the town's first experiment in banning vehicles to business premises" he wrote.

ENTERTAINMENT opportunities in Derby had also begun to change rapidly since the conclusion of the war. In a year-end review, the *Telegraph* noted that, since 1945, some 11 of the town's 18 cinemas had closed. However, the paper reported: "Bingo has succeeded where films failed." In 1961, several of the town's former cinemas reopened as bingo halls and even the beloved old Hippodrome "may welcome the New Year as a bingo hall".

The paper went on: "Down have come cinema screens; up have gone bingo boards with flashing lights, magic numbers and automatic ping-pong ball blowers."

No easy future for aero-engines – and an uncertain time for railways

LOCAL manufacturing industry enjoyed fairly steady progress in 1961. "In a year of many political and economic uncertainties, Derby district can show a balance sheet which compares favourably with other industrial centres, although it has not come through 1961 entirely unscathed" wrote the *Telegraph*'s industrial correspondent.

Although "no easy future can be foreseen in the aero-engine field", there were tremendous possibilities for new markets – in Europe, particularly if Britain's application to join the European Common Market were to be accepted – and the "Chinese market and prospects in the Far East generally". The correspondent noted that local firms had already been forward thinking in approaching new world markets.

His report ended on a note of caution, however, in particular for Derby's railway industries as the country awaited the conclusions of the Beeching Report, which was expected to revolutionise the rail system: "What the future holds for the railways only time – and Dr Beeching – will unfold".

"The sexiest man on television"

FORMER Bemrose School pupil, Eric Lander, was enjoying the height of his fame in 1961. Described as the "sexiest man on television", Lander received more fan mail than Clint Eastwood, who was then appearing in *Gunsmoke*. For two years Lander had starred in the popular crime series *No Hiding Place*, as sidekick to Raymond Francis's Detective Chief Superintendent Tom Lockhart.

Now Lander's character, Harry Baxter – promoted to detective inspector – was given his own series *Echo Four Two*. Based in Bow Street, Baxter's patch extended to the market at Covent Garden, to the Thames and into the West End – giving plenty of opportunity to discover a variety of storylines and characters.

However, due to an Equity strike, the planned 13-part series was never completed. The finished episodes were aired during the hiatus between two series of *No Hiding Place*, but the new series never captured the public's imagination. Perhaps they were now used to the hour-long American-style drama of *No Hiding Place* while *Echo Four Two* was a traditional 30-minute show. When it ended, Lander returned to the original series.

Meanwhile, Allestree's Alan Bates starred in the delightful *Whistle Down The Wind* alongside child actress Hayley Mills, whose mother, Mary Hayley Bell, had written the story. Described on its US posters as "A Story About Kids ... For Everyone!" the film was a charming tale of a little girl and her brother who discover a fugitive hiding on their father's farm. When she asks him who he is, the fugitive, played by Bates, is able only to mutter the words "Jesus Christ!" before passing into unconsciousness. The God-fearing children believe they have the Son of God in their barn and attempt to protect him.

Eventually the police, who are hunting him down for murder, find and arrest him.

Derbyshire cricket

DERBYSHIRE'S young wicketkeeper, Bob Taylor, made his first-class debut for the county against Sussex in June, standing in for the injured George Dawkes. That season, Taylor would play in 17 first class matches, taking an impressive 47 catches and making six stumpings. He would also boast a batting average of 11.8 runs – making a top score of 48 – not bad for an out-and-out wicketkeeper at the very beginning of his career.

It was a quietly impressive debut season, but once Taylor permanently took over from Dawkes the following season, he would continue playing for the county, and eventually his country, until his retirement in 1984. In total he would dismiss 1,304 batsmen for Derbyshire, and 1,649 in all first-class cricket, and break several records for his adopted county.

The previous month saw the much-anticipated visit of the Australian touring side – captained by Neil Harvey in place of the injured Richie Benaud – to Derbyshire. Derbyshire CCC's committee had improved facilities and ensured that extra seating was installed at Queen's Park in Chesterfield. Unfortunately, a weekend of heavy rain had drenched the pitch and play was delayed (ironically the weather was now fine and sunny) until 11.45am on the second of the scheduled three days. Only 22 overs were possible in 66 minutes of play – modern cricket fans might well raise en eyebrow at such a high over-rate – before the heavens opened again and the match was disappointingly abandoned.

INCLEMENT weather had been something of a feature in 1961. In January, persistent heavy rainfall had led to flooding in much of the county, and the year ended with icy, foggy conditions with rivers and lakes freezing over. The *Evening Telegraph*'s front page even featured a photograph of skaters on Allestree Lake; however council officials warned that the lakes and rivers were not safe for such activities.

Yet if the weather in 1961 was to prove problematic for householders, cricketers and those simply seeking a little outdoor fun, it was nothing compared to the conditions that Derbyshire folk would experience in 1962.

1962

A new vibrancy

ALTHOUGH the 1960s had yet to get into full swing, by 1962 Derby's youngsters were dancing to a new type of sound, with the 'Twist' one of the most popular dances. The year also saw some of pop music's hottest young stars visit the town. The seemingly ever-present controversy over Derby's modernisation programme continued – with the Inner Ring Road again the focus of attention. And, never mind that, for two weeks in October, the world stood on the brink of nuclear annihilation, the weather had its own frightening forces to throw at the county in 1962. There were even armed robberies.

The transformation of Derby – which is often blamed for the destruction of many old and lovely buildings, as well as for the disappearance of some of the original street plan – also brought a new vibrancy to the town. Although we now look back on what later came to be regarded as "white elephants", there was much excitement at the construction of two modern shopping precincts.

One was to be built on the site of the old Castlefields Mill, off London Road, and would eventually be given the decidedly unglamorous, and ultimately inaccurate, name, Main Centre.

At the other end of town, behind the Congregational Church on Victoria Street, work was under way to demolish a number of

The Main Centre shopping precinct off London Road. It later made way for the Westfield shopping centre.

Victoria Street Congregational Church stood on the corner of Victoria Street and Becket Well Lane.

buildings to make way for Duckworth Place – a state-of-the-art precinct with 20 shops and a drive-in rooftop car park for more than 100 cars.

The church itself and the old Black Prince cinema were among the many buildings sacrificed for the £250,000 development. The cinema had been constructed in 1910 as the Victoria Electric Theatre. From 1948, under the ownership of Edgar Duckworth, it changed its name from the Empire to the Black Prince. Entirely refurbished, complete with drawbridge-style main entrance and a redecorated auditorium, in 1954 it had become only the country's fourth independent cinema to boast Cinemascope. It had welcomed its last audiences in March 1960.

Even in 1962, the ongoing construction of Derby's Inner Ring Road was causing concern and debate among the town's residents. Both Alderman Alec Ling, and at least one reader of the *Evening Telegraph*, who had proudly signed himself "Petrol Burner", expressed their concern that the Town Council had fixed the wrong priorities and completed the wrong phases of the scheme ahead of more essential sections.

Work was, by then, under way on the Bradshaw Way section, to link it with the existing Traffic Street. "Petrol Burner" had complained particularly about the "acute rush-hour congestion" at Derby's notorious traffic "blackspot" in the Morledge and Corporation Street.

Asked by the *Evening Telegraph* to comment, the Borough Engineer explained that, while he was in agreement that the most important section – in terms of easing congestion – was that which would connect the Morledge with Nottingham Road, it was not yet possible to begin work on this "Central Way". First the Derby Canal, although long since abandoned, had to be officially closed by Parliament. At this point permission, and funds to complete the work, would be released to the Council.

But, while many were wanting a quick completion of the work, others feared for the future of many of Derby's most ancient byways and buildings, particularly those that lay in the path of the Inner Ring Road.

Perhaps these concerns were on the mind of Derby's new mayor, Stuart Harper, who wanted his year in office to be remembered for Derby becoming a "brighter" place. He wanted to see the town developed, beautified and "as far as is humanly possible, old and historic buildings preserved".

Improvements of a less controversial sort were announced at one of Derby's best-known hosiery mills. R. Rowley & Co Ltd, on Uttoxeter New Road, had just completed a total "rejuvenation" in anticipation of the increased trade opportunities that would exist, once Britain joined the European Common Market, which their directors believed was imminent. They were also advertising vacancies for overlockers, cutters, neck linkers, hand flat knitters and lockstitch machinists.

Derbyshire county policemen pictured with their vehicles in Bold Lane in 1962.

Leisure time

ON the whole, business in Derby was enjoying reasonable prosperity and, with younger folk now having a little more disposable income, the social scene had become ever more vibrant.

The Twist had taken the world, and Derby, by storm and, in February, the Trocadero Ballroom on Normanton Road hosted a Twist competition. Christine Wood and Janet Barber were the winners and received the Wyles Trophy for their efforts. Some eight months later, 17-year-old Janet, of Napier Street, and 18-year-old Lance Marr, of Crompton Street, won the local heat of a national Twist competition, along with a £10 prize and the chance to compete for the £100 national prize.

The "Big Star Show of 1962", which had been touring Britain throughout the year, visited the Gaumont on London Road in the spring. Its star was Billy Fury, whose hit records *Halfway to Paradise* and *Jealousy* had both made No 1 in the charts the previous year. Also on the tour was Eden Kane who had also had a No 1 – *Well I Ask You* – that year. Kane's early promise would not be entirely fulfilled and his younger brothers, Peter and Robin Sarstedt, would enjoy brief pop careers after Kane's had faded. Using his real name of Richard Sarstedt, Kane eventually became a regular television actor in the US. Appearing in a number of series, including several episodes of the various *Star Trek* series.

"Sophisticated" John Leyton, famous for his hit *Johnny Remember Me,* was the third big star to feature. Singing was his second career – Leyton had already made a name for himself as an actor, playing Ginger in the television series *Biggles.* Leyton would continue acting, and featured in many films, including *The Great Escape* in 1963 and *Krakatoa, East of Java* in 1969.

The star acts were supported by others still at the very start of their careers. Peter Jay and the Jaywalkers would have a hit later in 1962 with their version of *The Can Can.* Shane Fenton would enjoy two pop careers, one with his band the Fentones and one, in the 1970s, as the glam rock performer Alvin Stardust. Cockney Joe Brown completed the line-up.

In October, Billy Fury returned to the Gaumont, this time with Mike Sarne and Marty Wilde. "Wearing a sort of tweed suit," the *Evening Telegraph*'s reviewer noted, "Billy twisted and shook his hair over his eyes as he went through his top numbers. And he only had to give his audience that certain look to provoke a near riot and a bombardment of autograph books and flowers."

After the show "almost the whole cast went to a party at 1 West Street, Heanor, home of Mr Albert Hand, publisher of magazines." What a party that must have been!

Back in March, two lucky Derby girls had had the pleasure of meeting the country's top pop idol – Cliff Richard. The young rock 'n' roller had been appearing at the Gaumont, where he had been "showered with missiles of roses, chocolates, stuffed toys and love notes", and the Picture Edition of the *Evening Telegraph* showed four-year-old Yvonne Stone of Watson Street, and her 16-year-old sister, Marie, as the former sat on the pop star's knee in his dressing room.

Several locals enjoyed considerable success in 1962. Allestree's Alan Bates starred in the drama *A Kind of Loving*, while Chesterfield-born John Hurt, made both his professional stage (in *Infanticide in the House of Fred Ginger*) and cinema (*The Young and the Willing*) debuts. Another debutant, this time to television, was Buxton's Tim Brooke-Taylor, who appeared in *On the Braden Beat*.

Armed robbery

TODAY we almost take gun crime for granted. Over 50 years ago it was so rare as to make national news. In February 1962, however, in Derby, came two attempted armed robberies in two days. On 3 February, the *Evening Telegraph* reported that a man was under arrest after apparently pointing a gun at a wages clerk in Wilderslowe House on Osmaston Road, where the Hospital

Management Committee's finance department was based. He had demanded that the clerk fill his rucksack with money. However, most employees had already been paid and relatively little cash had been on the premises. The would-be robber had fled when confronted by staff and was arrested a short time later after an extensive police search. His automatic pistol and ammunition had been stolen from a local dealer, where he had posed as a prospective customer earlier that day.

Two days later, police were searching for another armed robber. This time, the Normanton Road Filling Station had been the target. Again, no money was taken and the proprietor, Mrs Pauline Williams, was able to give police a good description, although the man had worn a scarf over his face.

The start of a dreadful winter

BY the end of 1962, it was the weather that was making the daily headlines. The year had got off to a stormy start. At the beginning of February, a violent gale lashed the county.

The *Evening Telegraph* reported: "Roofs were ripped off, chimney stacks crashed, trees fell across roads and vehicles were overturned."

The roof was lifted off Etwall County Primary School, and, at Allestree Rec, a wooden pavilion was torn from its foundations, the pieces landing in a neighbouring garden. Windows were smashed at Henry Cavendish School in Breadsall; lorries were blown over on the road between Coxbench and Kilburn. Many roads – including Ashbourne Road, Queensway, Enfield Road and Radbourne Lane – were blocked because of fallen trees. Double-decker buses swayed dangerously. One Egginton couple were grateful to have evacuated their new bungalow, as a large beech tree fell on to it, effectively slicing it in half.

But even this great storm was just a foretaste of the awful weather that was to hit Britain. Winter had been late setting in, with little sign of it until early December. Then, three weeks of fog and near-freezing temperatures had teased the county, but it was not until Boxing Day that a band of snow, sweeping south from Scotland, had stalled over southern Britain and brought a belated white Christmas to the county. The snow that would become a feature of life for the next few months had arrived.

1963

The coldest winter for 168 years

DRAMATIC new changes to the centre of Derby, the possible effects of the Beeching Report, two dramatic fires, and the coldest winter for nearly two centuries – they all served to make 1963 one of Derby's most memorable years.

The winter of 1963 was reckoned to be the coldest since 1795. Day after day throughout January and February, daytime temperatures barely crept above freezing, with nightfall bringing bitterly cold conditions. Rivers and lakes froze over and there was a constant layer of ice and compacted snow on the ground. Derbeians began to wonder what the town's pavement's actually looked like.

Although Derbyshire fared better than many other parts of Great Britain, the snow that had fallen at Christmas did not melt away until March and, as fine layers of snowfall fell on top of existing ice for weeks on end, conditions underfoot became utterly treacherous.

But the bitter cold was, perhaps, the greatest threat. With none but the most comfortable of houses enjoying the benefits of central heating, there was little respite from the cold. Clothing, of course, owed little to the high-tech weather-beaters of more modern times.

Each person might expect to own one winter coat, probably made of wool, and almost certainly with no specialised padding or thermal properties. Add to that a scarf, a woolly hat and a pair of woollen gloves or mittens, and the average Briton of 1963 had all the protection he or she could muster against the bitterest weather for 200 years.

Sporting activities, inevitably, fell victim to the extreme conditions. Between 22 December 1962 and 2 March 1963, Second Division Derby County could play only one League game – a 2-2 draw with Sunderland at the Baseball Ground in late February – while the home FA Cup third-round tie against Peterborough United, originally scheduled for 5 January, was postponed six times before the game could be played on 4 February, when the Rams won. The football authorities had no option but to extend the season, which in those days usually finished in late April, and Derby did not play their last game until 18 May.

Eventually, as they days grew longer, a gradual thaw set in. Weather experts declared 6 March as the first day in 1963 when the entire country was frost-free. Of course, with the thaw, came flooding. The *Evening Telegraph* reported: "Now Floods As Rain Melts Snow – Roads Affected". At Matlock Green a "freak inundation" flooded several properties as water from thawing ice backed up behind a fallen tree trunk in Bentley Brook. But any disruption was now limited and life could return largely to normal.

Derby gets ready for the Common Market

THE possibility of Britain joining the Common Market was both an exciting and uncertain one for many local companies. Directors of Aiton & Co Ltd, which had operated from a large works on Stores Road since 1907, had decided to ensure that their company was ready for the challenges and opportunities that lay ahead.

On 18 March, they announced that a section of the factory was to close as part of the firm's reorganisation. It was hoped that this would also allow for expansion of the business to "produce steel pipework in view of the expanding demand for power plant all over the world". Bosses estimated that only 40 of the 800 employees would be forced into redundancy and they invited unions to assist in finding alternative employment for those unlucky few.

The *Telegraph* reported that directors had stated: "To make it quicker for the men to get other jobs, they will be able to leave at any time during the next six weeks." Nevertheless, the men were unlikely to be able to walk into another job straight away.

More worrying news came with the publication of the long-anticipated Beeching Report into the national railway network. It called for the removal of one-third of passenger lines and the closure of more than 2,000 stations, including those in Derby at Friar Gate and on Nottingham Road, and those serving Belper, Borrowash, Clay Cross, Matlock Bath, Ambergate, Buxton, Darley Dale, Duffield, Langley Mill and Eastwood, Repton and Willington, and several others.

In Derby, there were fears that the plan, should it be followed through in its entirety, would "mean eventually a complete breakdown of the railway system", a point which was raised in the local paper by Mr R. W. Brothill of Valley Road, Littleover, a trustee of the National Union of Railwaymen. And, of course, there were also fears that fewer railway lines and stations would mean fewer locomotives and carriages – a possibility that would impact significantly on two of the town's major employers – the Loco Works and Carriage and Wagon works.

Sad end for much-loved Assembly Rooms

ECONOMIC concerns aside, there was a great deal of anticipation and debate over future developments of Derby in 1963. However, plans got off to a bad start in mid-February when the old and much-loved Assembly Rooms suffered severe fire damage. The blaze, which seemed to have been started by

The 18th-century Assembly Rooms graced the Market Place until they were badly damaged by fire in 1963.

The beautiful ceiling of Derby's 18th-century Assembly Rooms was damaged in the 1963 fire. The building had to be demolished.

an electrical fault in the amplifying system, destroyed much of the roof. Immediate concerns were to safely remove the heavy ventilator, some 6ft in diameter, which was dangling precariously from the charred roof timbers.

The *Telegraph* warned: "Roof of famous building may have to be removed entirely." But no-one had realised the extent of the damage. It was eventually decided that the building was lost and for many years its façade was wrapped in safety scaffolding, before being removed, piece by piece, to be re-erected at the tramway museum at Crich.

Another town centre fire at the end of May, this time at the Drill Hall in Becket Street, proved no less dramatic. Although the hall rarely had ammunition stored inside it, the very morning that the fire broke out, several boxes of rifle bullets had been delivered in preparation for an exercise. Attempts to extinguish the blaze were "hampered by exploding ammunition" and local residents were forced to evacuate their homes until the fire brigade, who were able to salvage several boxes of ammunition, declared the area safe.

Dramatic plans for a new town centre

PROPOSED alterations to Derby's townscape of a more deliberate kind were unveiled in July. The dramatic proposals would see much of the old townscape either swept away or dwarfed by new buildings and even an elevated roadway. Architects' models showed pedestrians carrying shopping beneath the hulk of a vast overhead road that was to begin in the Morledge, where a ramp would take it to first-floor level, along Albert Street, and into Victoria Street and Green Lane.

Another such road was proposed for East Street and along St Peter's Churchyard. Benefits might have included being able to shop "free from traffic worries", but the horrors of such an ugly behemoth cutting right through some of Derby's oldest streets, obliterating the townscape and leaving shoppers to contend with the dark, dismal pedestrian lanes beneath, apparently proved too depressing even for the most adventurous and forward-thinking town planner. Thankfully, only a single elevated service road, across East Street, ever made its way from planning office to town centre.

Several other aspects of the plan did come to fruition, although in some cases not for several decades, and in others only in modified forms. A new pedestrianised, outdoor shopping precinct was proposed, complete with underground car park, in the Eagle Street area of the town. Above the shops at Exchange Street, offices were to be built, and at The Spot, a modern hotel was to be constructed. A new home for the Open Market in the Morledge was to be built, between the new precinct and the Morledge, and a public house was to be built to serve the market.

The elevated road that would have taken traffic through Derby's town centre, past the former Northcliffe House, along Albert Street and Victoria Street, and then turned up Green lane.

The Market Place was to be completely pedestrianised and a wide five-storey office complex was to fill in the gap on the west side of the square, between the Guildhall and the ruin of the Assembly Rooms, which it was anticipated, would be fully restored. Beneath the office block, a restaurant, showrooms, a public house and market stalls would be constructed. It was suggested, too, that a pedestrian bridge be built from the office block to the Council House.

Opposite the Guildhall, a brand new concert hall was proposed, again with shops beneath it. On the Morledge, between East Street and Albert Street, a modern "departmental" store was suggested.

Derbeians, of course, had their own ideas on how to improve the town centre. Back in February, D. Beath of Uttoxeter Road had written to the *Evening Telegraph* suggesting new traffic measures that could "provide the greatest amenity for most citizens". He, or she, suggested that the council spend no more public money on new roads and parking spaces in Derby; the private cars, and non-stop commercial vehicles, be banned from the town centre; and that speed restrictions of 20mph be placed on permitted traffic. D. Beath also proposed the abolition of traffic lights and "other obstructions to the steady flow of pedestrians and vehicles" and, to make the streets more pedestrian-friendly, the widening of pavements and the lowering of curbs.

Another suggestion, which would no doubt have found favour with shoppers, if not with the council who had to foot the bill, was the instigation of "frequent short services of conductorless front-doored trolley buses on which no fare will be taken between Friar Gate, the Post Office, Market Place and the Bus Station". Modern shoppers, and environmentalists, might have preferred the council take more note of these suggestions than they did those of the town planners.

Saxon graves at Little Chester – and an escalator for Marks and Spencer

MARKS & Spencer, meanwhile, placed a prominent advertisement in the *Evening Telegraph* to announce their own latest improvement. "Marks and Spencer announce the installation of an ESCALATOR to the New and Enlarged Food Section on the Upper Sales Floor."

If Derby's ancient origins seemed a long way from all this modernisation, evidence of earlier habitation was uncovered at Little Chester. Several fifth to seventh-century Saxon graves were discovered during excavations at the old Roman Derventio settlement.

IN December there was drama for a group of local children, when a school bus was involved in an accident. Fifty rugby enthusiasts from Bemrose School, on their way to play and watch rugby in London, were involved in a crash on the A5 near – ironically – Rugby. Although nine boys were taken to hospital, none suffered serious injury. "Everything," said headmaster Dr W. R. C. Chapman, "is going happily."

By mid-December icy conditions had returned, although most Derbeians realised they were unlikely to prove as difficult as the previous winter. They hoped for better things in 1964.

1964

Markeaton Hall to be demolished

IN 1964, early plans for the demolition of Markeaton Hall were met with a public outcry so fierce that the town's Parks Committee temporarily withdrew its recommendation. The demise of Darley Hall in 1962, and the Assembly Rooms in 1963, both under the watch of the council, had left Derbeians determined not to lose any more of their favourite buildings.

While South-East Derbyshire Rural Council were busy gathering resources to purchase the Elvaston Castle estate for use as a public open space, it was unclear what Derby's council had planned for the old hall given to the town in 1929 by Mrs Emily Mundy.

Councillor J. E. Clay, chairman of the Parks Committee, would not be drawn publicly on the possibilities under discussion, or their costs: "I don't want to anticipate anything. It would be wrong for me to give any figures at all at present, or any idea of what is likely to take place".

In the possession of the Corporation for 35 years, Markeaton Hall had been allowed to fall into disrepair following wartime use by the military. By 1964, the condition of the hall had deteriorated dramatically. The debate on its future continued

Markeaton Hall in all its glory. The council did not maintain it and one of Derby's finest buildings was eventually demolished.

for some time, with one alderman even declaring the hall to be the "Shibboleth of the oppressive capital-owning classes."

Eventually, perhaps through an inability or unwillingness to find and fund an appropriate new use for it, Markeaton Hall was decreed beyond repair and the entire structure demolished. All that remained was the stable block, Pickford's lovely orangery and a range of rather brutal and functional Second World War army buildings. Many Derbeians were worried that the Town Council seemed almost determined to allow all its treasures to fall to pieces.

"Bring your car into Derby town centre"

ONE thing that the council was not indecisive about was the relentless modernisation of the town centre. In August, the *Evening Telegraph* reported: "It will soon be possible to bring your car into Derby town centre, park it, do your shopping, have lunch followed by a game of ten-pin bowling, then go to the pictures and, if you wish, stay the night in a luxury hotel, and have the car filled all on one site".

The site in question was the land between Victoria, Colyear, Macklin and Becket Streets. The Scarsdale Arms Hotel in Colyear Street was just the latest building to be demolished to make way for the project. As well as a multi-storey car park, filling stations, and a high-rise hotel, a brand-new "discotheque club" was to be built, boasting a "luxurious coffee bar and ballroom, with stereophonic sound system".

With the brand new neighbouring Duckworth Square shopping precinct already welcoming its first customers, "gay new fashion store" John Bryan took out a full-page advertisement in the *Evening Telegraph* recommending the "ease of precinct shopping". Its fashions were, it proclaimed: "Especially designed for the YOUNG and the YOUNG IN HEART"

Indeed, reflecting the nation's growing disposable income, there were an increasing number of such advertisements for fashionable clothing and, in particular, for state-of-the-art household appliances.

Telefusion offered a "big screen" branded television receiver for just 6s 11d per week rental. It also advertised "slot televisions" with pay-per-view meters.

One of the new programmes that customers might well have been tuning in to was ATV's new soap opera *Crossroads*. And Derbeians had extra reason to take an interest in the motel-based drama: one of its stars, and the actress given the honour of the series' first lines, was 21-year-old Derby-born Jane Rossington. It was a simple enough start for an actress who, through her character Jill Richardson, would endure three marriages, countless love affairs, childbirth, drug addiction, mental breakdown and severe depression.

Derby-born racing driver Reg Parnell died in 1964.

Local sporting legends ... and PJ Proby fails to turn up

THE sporting world celebrated the career of Whitwell-born snooker and billiards legend Joe Davies, who retired from his sports as perhaps the greatest player of all time. Davies won 15 world snooker titles and 10 world or UK billiards championships. He had made 687 snooker century breaks and 83 billiard breaks of over 1,000. Sports fans also mourned the premature death of Derby-born Findern resident Reg Parnell, who had been one of the world's most promising racing drivers before the Second World War halted his career. In the post-war years, Parnell had become one of the most successful Formula 1 team managers in motor racing history.

For those who preferred to get their entertainment live and in person, the much-anticipated PJ Proby concert at the King's Hall on Queen Street appeared to fit the bill. However, because the controversial American star "did not turn up" for a concert in Croydon the previous night, there was speculation and confusion on the day of the Derby concert. In the end Proby did not appear and the promoters had to refund £600 to disappointed Derbeians.

Derbyshire railwaymen's jobs threatened

IN September 1964, Derby Friargate railway station was closed to passengers. January had already brought news that in the north of the county, the Rowsley marshalling yards were to

Into the 1960s, the "Friargate line" still crossed the River Derwent near Darley Park.

St Andrew's good depot and, in the distance, St Andrew's Church on London Road. By the late 1960s the days of both were numbered.

close, threatening some 600 railwaymen's jobs. The villages, which had grown up around the yards, faced an uncertain future because an estimated 400 families depended on the railways for a living.

Rowsley had been an important junction linking the lines from the Derbyshire and Nottinghamshire coalfields to the northern industrial cities.

As the railway station for Chatsworth, Rowsley had also played host to visiting dignitaries like Edward VII, Prime Minister William Gladstone and various ambassadors. Union officials scheduled an urgent meeting in Matlock, and local MP, Aidan Crawley, contacted British Railways and the unions to enquire what redundancy provisions had been made.

Time for new traditions?

FOR most people, however, the year brought happy times, and the social calendar was packed with traditional annual celebrations like the many May Festivals held by churches and local communities. The Picture Edition of the *Evening Telegraph* featured that run by the Derby Band of Hope. Their festival was held at the Central Hall where 16-year-old Jill Poxon was crowned May Queen.

Perhaps surprisingly to modern Derbeians, the local Society of Orangemen marched through the centre of town, from Bass's Rec to the Market Place. It was the first such march since 1959.

Traditions might have been strong throughout the town and county, but as the year closed and 1965 approached, to paraphrase the words of the Bob Dylan song of that year – the times they were a-changin'. A Picture Edition of the *Evening Telegraph* featured the pupils of Rosehill Secondary and Hardwick Girls' Schools where, the paper noted: "Coloured pupils settle down in Derby schools". It was time for a modern Derby to create some new traditions.

1965

It was all about travel and fashion

DEBATES about more town centre improvements, complaints about a lack of fashionable clothing in local shops, and sporting controversy were among the stories making the headlines in Derbyshire in 1965, while a last-minute hiccup at the region's new airport very nearly turned into an April Fool's joke as the Ministry of Aviation withheld its license.

The opening of East Midlands Airport at Castle Donington had been scheduled for 1 April 1965, but snow in early March had put work – which had, thus far, been going well – behind schedule and, in the days leading up to the opening, a vital piece of machinery had broken down. Fortunately, most of the required work was completed by mid-afternoon on the day in question, but a licence to commence daylight flying only was issued; an accident with the runway lighting meant no night flights for the time being.

In anticipation of the opening, B & H International Travel Services had already been offering trips from East Midlands. For just 21 guineas, Derbeians could spend eight days in either Ostend or Blankenberge. Indeed, foreign travel was becoming the norm for many local families. The same agents were advertising several European holidays, such as a 10-day coach tour through Austria for 17½ guineas, or a 15-day Grand Tour of Italy for 39½ guineas.

For young people, of course, following the latest fashions had become very important. The *Evening Telegraph* devoted one page every week – *Young Ones* – to this growing interest in pop music and fashion trends. Writer Liz Thompson, disappointed at the lack of truly fashionable clothing available in the town, described her frustration. Among the items not available in Derby were "crochet sweaters and berets, summery baby bonnets, printed suits and trouser suits, keyhole backed gloves, lacy stockings, battle dress tops, and scalloped trims".

This lack of variety was causing embarrassment for the "up-to-the-minute girl" who ran the risk of turning up to a party in the same dress as several of her friends. The problem, it seemed, was that the national fashion chains did not think high-fashion items would sell well in Derby: "The Londoner's image of the Midland girl as a plump, unfashionable country pudding has persisted far too long!" complained Ms Thompson.

In lieu of a trendy boutique, Derby's Co-operative Society did its best to provide young women with clothing that was at least stylish and affordable, which it showcased at an in-store fashion show viewed by the Mayor and Mayoress. Displayed on the catwalk were shorter length spring coats, sleeveless dresses with broderie anglaise frills, and two-piece, stripy beachwear. However, if the Co-op had intended to attract youngsters into its store, there was little evidence of that particular demographic in the fashion show audience.

According to the *Evening Telegraph*, however, some younger Derbeians were more than happy at the supply of the "latest thing in slippers" – they were decorated in "Dalek motifs" from the BBC Television serial *Doctor Who*.

One local girl who was certainly a keen follower of fashion was Belper-born actress Suzi Kendall. The "honey blonde with blue eyes" had been a photographic model before successfully auditioning for a role in Christopher Miles' new film *Up Jumped A Swagman*, which was about to be released. Having filmed more than 30 television commercials and studied acting for six months, Miss Kendall was keen to begin her new cinematic career.

The Harold Rhodes Affair

IN sport, as the opening game of the South African tour of England got under way at Queen's Park, Chesterfield, there was great tension. Many people in Britain did not welcome the

ELIZABETH LANE, who had served as Recorder of the Borough of Derby for two years, became the first woman High Court Judge in Britain. She had already paved a remarkable career path. In 1946, she had been the first woman to argue a murder appeal in the House of Lords, and had become the first female county court judge in 1962. She was also the first female divorce commissioner and the first woman deputy chairperson of the Inner London Sessions.

arrival of cricketers from a country with such a poor human rights record. As the match began, anti-apartheid demonstrators picketed the picturesque park. But it was events inside the ground, and surrounding an Englishman, not a South African, that was to dominate proceedings.

Derbyshire fast bowler Harold Rhodes was no stranger to controversy. Five years earlier, and also against the South Africans, an umpire had questioned the legality of his whippy bowling action. Even though the fuss had by now largely died down, the intervening years had seen further occasional accusations of "chucking". But, in 1965, Rhodes had enjoyed one of his best starts to a season and there was great anticipation that he was on the verge of being selected once more for the England team. But again, amid all the political argument, Rhodes' technique was called into question. Square-leg umpire Syd Buller called him twice in successive balls and he was forced to complete his over with ineffectual slow leg-breaks. Things turned nastier during the tea interval as Buller was subjected to a torrent of abuse from Derbyshire supporters and even needed a police escort to his hotel.

Eventually, after his bowling action was filmed and analysed by experts, it would be revealed that Rhodes had an unusual,

Derbyshire fast bowler Harold Rhodes wearing an arm splint before being filmed to show that he did not "throw" the ball.

and quite natural, hyperextension of his elbow joint. He was certainly no cheat.

A new civic centre for Derby?

IN Derby there was much discussion about the location for the town's proposed civic centre. The intention was to provide a modern venue for concerts and other public events which would go some way to replacing the burnt-out old Assembly Rooms, which still stood at one end of the Market Place. A consortium, which had purchased most of the property on the north side of the square, proposed selling the land to the council to build the civic centre and leasing back shop units which would be built at street level.

However, many local people, such as Councillor T. D. Barlow, felt it would be more appropriate to build the centre at Markeaton Park, particularly since it was also intended to host sporting events there. But again there was opposition. Councillor W. A. C. Burrows expressed concerns that "three-quarters of the town's population would need to use two buses to get to Markeaton Park", and that a civic centre should be in the middle of the town it was meant to serve. Another councillor suggested that the centre be built on the banks of the Derwent, on land that was due to be vacated by the open market – itself scheduled to be relocated on the other side of the Morledge.

There was even more debate about the fate of the old Assembly Rooms itself. Some favoured demolishing it, others restoring it, and many more incorporating it into any new structure. It seemed the only thing that could be agreed on was the need for action to be taken.

Somewhere new to live

MANY Derbeians saw the opening of the town's only "skyscraper" – the new Rivermead House council flats on Bath Street – as a horrible vision of the future. Although the 94 flats were provided with all "mod cons", and the block was served by four lifts, the council had encountered great difficulty in persuading people to accept accommodation there. They had been forced to look quite a way down the housing list for willing occupants.

Privately owned housing was on the increase and there were new estates being built right across the district. Particularly popular, it seemed, were modern bungalows. Estate agent Frank Innes advertised a "recently built, attractively designed detached chalet bungalow" on a corner plot at Borrowash for £3,450. The new home boasted a spacious hall, large lounge with feature fireplace, breakfast kitchen and three double bedrooms as well as a garage and a garden. A three-bedroomed palisaded house in Palmerston Street was offered for £1,750. One of the most expensive properties on sale was a "very superior modern" semi-detached house on Station Road, Mickleover. This home provided three bedrooms, outhouses, a workshop, brick garage and a large garden with patios and lawns, and was listed for sale at £4,500.

Existing Derby householders were expressing concern at the council's decision to add fluoride to local water supplies. C. H. Parker wrote to the *Evening Telegraph* to complain of the "total disregard for the fundamental right of the individual to decide whether or not he shall partake of any medicine or drug". While W. H. Beattie wondered: "what effect … it will have on our flower and vegetable gardens?"

In June, the government announced plans to build the British Railways Design Research and Development Centre in Derby. The £2.25 million scheme would ensure that "Derby will lead world as rail scientific centre". But there was also cause for concern in the railway industry as the next phase of proposals to scale down railway services was announced.

Into the future – "hundreds of giant trains"

THE *Evening Telegraph* reported that British Railways predicted that by 1984 "hundreds of giant trains would be hurtling non-

Traffic negotiating Mansfield Road in December 1965, when many streets in the Little Chester area were inundated after the River Derwent burst its banks.

stop at 70 mph and more, over a streamlined network of trunk routes, connecting the main centres". Concerns were raised because Derby, previously a major railway hub for lines from all directions, was predicted to be only a stop on one of those major routes – the one that connected the North-East with the South-West. Lines connecting the North-East and the North-West with London would use other routes. The streamlining would, it was claimed, increase demand on both passenger and freight services. Progress, as inevitable as it was, would clearly come at a cost.

1966

Death of a veteran politician

AS the New Year dawned, Derby was buzzing with anticipation for the forthcoming FA Cup third-round home tie against Manchester United. A chance to see the Rams take on the likes of Bobby Charlton, Denis Law and George Best persuaded thousands of fans to queue for tickets for hours on a bitterly cold Sunday. The *Evening Telegraph* reported that the queues stretched "four and five deep along both sides of Colombo Street, Shaftesbury Crescent, Vulcan Street, Harrington Street and as far as Holcombe Street". Local shops cashed in and reported their best Sunday trading for some years. But Rams fans, like Mr W. Billing of Slater Avenue, was "well worth it," even if the Rams eventually lost 5-2.

Meanwhile, the death of 95-year-old Alderman William Raynes gave the *Evening Telegraph* cause to look back on the former mayor's many decades of service to the town. Active in the trades unions since 1897, Raynes had made six attempts to stand for the town council before being successful in 1911. That year he also helped to found Derby Labour Party and, in 1921, he became the town's first Labour mayor. For many years, he stood as an agent for local MP, Jimmy Thomas, and himself served as local MP during two short spells – in 1923 and between 1929 and 1931. But it was his service to Derby Town Council for which Raynes would be best remembered. When he became a freeman of the borough in the 1950s, he had commented: "I have watched the development of this town from the days when it was a country market town of third-rate importance to its present proud position as one of the most enterprising and successful industrial centres in the county. I am proud to have been allowed to have take some little part in shaping its destiny."

Certainly, Raynes' contribution had been more than "little", for he had overseen some of the town's major improvements – the Flood Prevention Scheme and the building of the Power Station on Full Street among them – and he had been a prime mover in the construction of the Ring Road; Raynesway had been named in his honour. Raynes had also proposed the entire rebuilding of the town centre, in order that key landmarks – the

Cathedral and Friar Gate railway bridge, for example – might be observed unobstructed from some distance away. While many might have cringed at the mass destruction Raynes' proposals encouraged, none could doubt his passion for the development and improvement of his hometown.

A new school for Derby – or an old one reinvented?

WHETHER William Raynes approved of the extremely modern new premises for Derby's oldest educational establishment was not recorded. The ancient Derby School – founded in 1554 – had resided in St Helen's House for the best part of a century, having relocated from its original home on St Peter's Churchyard, but the old mansion was now proving quite unsuitable for a modern school.

As the new academic year began, the entire school moved to its state-of-the-art, purpose-built modern, tower block new site at Moorway Lane, to the south-east of the town. It was quite a contrast to the earlier town centre locations; some rather pastoral photographs in the *Evening Telegraph* showed cows grazing on land surrounding the new school. Designed and planned in the Borough Architect's Department, the steel-framed structure had cost £290,000 to build. Some of the greatest improvements were the new playing fields and sports facilities – elements that had been lacking at St Helen's House. However, until the turf had properly settled, pupils continued to use playing fields at Parker's Piece on City Road for outdoor sporting activities. Cricket practice nets, rugby fives courts and seven hard tennis courts were all completed.

The school buildings themselves consisted of a three-storey teaching block that formed three sides of an internal quadrangle, with the other side comprising administration and staff accommodation. Beyond that lay an "assembly, dining and gymnasium block" and classrooms for woodwork and metalwork lessons. The school was furnished with several science laboratories, in particular a biology lab that had "closed circuit television for demonstrations".

Many local firms were proud to announce their involvement with such a prestigious project. Bennett's of Irongate had provided architectural ironmongery; Barons' Landscape Ltd of Borrowash were preparing the playing fields and landscaping; Gizzonio Bros of Littleover had produced a school crest in mosaic tiling at the entrance; and Derby Glass had installed the enormous number of glazed panels.

Market celebrations

DURING 1966, the town council took the decision to open the Morledge market on Tuesdays, giving Derby three market days in total. After just one week, Mr A. E. Whittall, general manager of Derby Corporation Markets Department, pronounced it a resounding success. Some 230 stalls had opened and Mr Whittall was confident that, trade being so profitable, the Tuesday market would be running at "100 per cent" within weeks.

Derby's Market Hall, meanwhile, was celebrating 100 years in operation. Among those who placed celebratory advertisements in support of the *Evening Telegraph*'s feature were Paul's "the old reliable drapers" who promoted their hosiery, cosmetics and "the cheapest and best quality NYLON OVERALLS in Derby". J. R. M. Theaker & Son were proud to celebrate their own 50th year in the Market Hall and boasted of their potted meat and salmon paste: "Need we say more!"

Bowdens biscuit, cake and sweet specialists had "been in Derby Market for 75 years" and one of the largest stallholders was fruitier Joe Woodhouse, who also had greengroceries at the Morledge and Allenton markets, as well as on The Spot and at Alvaston. Bensims of Blackpool advertised the "finest selection of giftware, including watches, clocks, jewellery, china and Venetian glassware".

More multicultural

MODERN Derby was, of course, becoming even more multicultural. In January, the *Evening Telegraph* reported as Derby's Indian community mourned the death of their Prime Minister Lal Bahadur Shastri. Five hundred Sikh workers at the Qualcast factory at Sunnyhill held a memorial service in the works canteen. And in December, the newspaper covered the month-long Islamic festival of Ramadan by reporting that the Derby Muslim Society, based at the mosque at 54 Dairyhouse Road, had appointed Haji Mohammad Mahmood as Iman for the celebrations.

Goodbye to a pint of Offiler's

IN September, one of Derby's traditional companies, Offiler's Brewery, closed down. It had been founded at the Vine Inn on Whitaker Street in 1877, and the current works – at Ambrose Street – had been in operation since 1884. New owners, Charrington United Breweries, which had taken over the previous year, had decided that it was simply not economically viable to replace the machinery, and rebuild or modernise the premises to modern standards. With its demise, one of the last vestiges of an ancient Derby industry was lost. It would not be renewed until the advent of microbreweries at pubs like the Brunswick.

Festive entertainment

AS Christmas neared, local pubs and clubs placed their advertisements for the festive period. Although at least one *Evening Telegraph* writer had predicted that "last year's craze of folk music" was giving way to the new discotheques – "French for record technique" the paper helpfully informed readers – there was little evidence of the town's most popular nightspots installing "ultra-violet lights".

The dinner-dance was by far the most popular form of Christmas entertainment. Such events were offered at the

Balmoral Club on Charnwood Street, and the Curzon Club on Duckworth Square, where "Christmas at the Curzon" consisted of a turkey dinner and raffle, followed by an "all-star cabaret", for just two guineas.

At the Locarno on Babington Lane – formerly the Grand Theatre – there was to be "General Dancing" to their resident groups, the Dave Allen Band and the Jerry Vincent Trio. On Christmas Eve there was a gala ball, and on Boxing Day a "Starlight Ball" from just after midnight to 4am. The Rialto on Osmaston Road offered a "Gala Beat Night" with Alan B. Curtis and the Tumblers. At Dino's Club and Casino on Upper Boundary Road there was a "sing song night and dancing with the Tom Chamberlain Trio". The Havana Club on Uttoxeter New Road featured Keene and his band, and Count Campbell, while The Clouds on London Road advertised a performance by new band "Shotgun Express".

Although this group was only together for a few months, several of their members went on to greater things. Lead singer Beryl Marsden, considered Liverpool's answer to Brenda Lee, appeared alongside future stadium filler Rod Stewart, and Mick Fleetwood, later to co-found Fleetwood Mac. For those who preferred their entertainment a little more down-to-earth, the Bell & Castle on Burton Road advertised "Betty with the Gang". Further out of town, at the Newton Park Hotel at Newton Solney, there was to be a Grand Festival Buffet and Dance to the Maurice Harper Quartet. While every Saturday night in the hotel's Gillies Room, grills and smoked fish could be enjoyed while listening to folk pair Miggi & Jim.

For those preferring to celebrate the festive season at home, the family-friendly Co-operative Society advertised a special saving of 7s 6d when buying a bottle of Benito Cream Sherry "from Spain" with Renbard Orange Squash.

Of course, there were many children's parties too. The offspring of workers at the Carriage & Wagon Works' "S" Shop were treated to games and a visit by Santa. The 240 children of employees of the St Mary's Goods Depot at Chester Green attended a party at the Railway Institute where they, too, were visited by Father Christmas, and entertained by the pop group, The Generation, while the children of members of the Alvaston branch of the Royal British Legion enjoyed a cinema trip.

For those unable to get out and about, the Derby Transport Ambulance and Nursing Division of the St John Ambulance chauffeured more than 70 housebound people to a party at the Grange Hall, Littleover, where they were given tea and entertained by the Good Companions.

Something the entire family could enjoy was the good old pantomime. Derby Playhouse in Sacheverel Street presented every little girl's favourite story *Cinderella*. Film actor James Hayter starred and up-and-coming actress Lynda Baron – now more famous as Nurse Gladys Emmanuel in Ronnie Barker's *Open All Hours* – appeared as Prince Charming.

1967

The loss of some much-loved landmarks

MANY Derbeians were deeply unhappy that the on-going construction of the Inner Ring Road necessitated the destruction of one of the most beautiful parts of Derby: St Alkmund's Church and its churchyard, Derby's only Georgian square.

St Alkmund's was Derby's oldest Christian site, predating the town itself. Demolition work revealed several "lost" treasures, like the tombstone of Derby's most famous artist, Joseph Wright, together with several skulls and hundreds of bones beneath the church floor. A huge, highly ornamented stone Saxon coffin was also discovered. St Alkmund's Sarcophagus, as it became known after the Saxon king believed buried in it, now resides in Derby

Museum. It was clearly made for someone of great status, but some modern experts believe it was for another, nameless but significant, elder.

Other areas, too, were under threat. In July, the Government gave the go-ahead for the "Derby Central Development". Part of this was the long-awaited shopping precinct that had been proposed several years earlier. Comprising shops, a market, offices, flats and car parking, it was to cover some 16 acres of the Eagle Street area. The redevelopment of the Market Place, where a civic hall, shops and multi-storey car park were to be built, formed another part.

Around the corner, another of Derby's grandest buildings was destroyed. No 36 Cornmarket was once Devonshire House, the Derby townhouse of the Cavendish family. Originally owned by William Cavendish, the second son of Bess of Hardwick, in 1750 it had been rebuilt to a design by Joseph Pickford. In order for a new, brutally modern, department store to be built, five of the original nine bays had to be demolished.

The future of Derby's Guildhall, by contrast, was assured. It was needed by the expanding Borough Council, who had grown out of their purpose-built Council House. The Guildhall was to house Derby Corporation Omnibus Department, which had been administered from the Council House, while staff facilities had been provided at the former civic restaurant in Tenant Street.

The Health Department was to move to Castlefields in the Main Centre, and the Children's Office was to relocate to King's Chambers in Queen Street. The old Weights and Measures building, next to the Guildhall, was also to be put to council use. The combined cost of adapting all the buildings and moving the departments was estimated to be in the region of just under £40,000, considerably less than the cost of building a new Council House.

The mock Tudor-fronted Horse and Trumpet pub in Full Street was one of the many familiar buildings to disappear from the centre of Derby in the 1960s.

In October, Derby's policemen had their hands full when a lorry carrying 2,000 live chickens tipped over as it travelled along Albert Street. The poultry was being transported from Hull to the Dove Valley processing plant at Ashbourne. According to reports, the "chickens were packed 12 to a crate, piled eight high".

Electoral changes

THE electoral system in Derby was also to undergo great changes. In December, the Home Secretary approved a request that Derby be divided into 18 wards. All 16 existing aldermen were to retire and, at a new election, three councillors would be elected for each of the new wards, after which 18 aldermen would be chosen. Such sweeping changes were certainly necessary. The absorption of several surrounding villages – including Littleover,

Mickleover and Sinfin – within the Borough boundaries would increase the local population by an estimated 60,000 people.

Policing in the county was changing too, with the amalgamation of the Derby Borough Police, headquartered in Full Street, and the Derbyshire Constabulary, which occupied premises in St Mary's Gate.

Drug culture

IT was the apparent increase in drug-related crime that was really concerning Derbeians. In August, the *Evening Telegraph* reported a magistrates' hearing in which two youths had been found guilty of smoking cannabis – "Indian Hemp" the reporter had usefully explained – in a toilet at The Clouds nightclub. The miscreants were each fined £50.

Evening Telegraph columnist "Albert Street" voiced his own concerns. "What is the truth about teenage drug-taking in Derby and Derbyshire?" he asked. He questioned whether Derbeians weren't being worried unnecessarily. However, the new Derby County and Borough Police had established a special section to deal with vice and drugs and, if there was no serious problem, Albert Street wondered, why then the need for a specialist squad?

In February, the *Evening Telegraph* had carried an article in which a Derby probation officer had stated that many Derby youngsters had begun taking drugs because it was regarded as fashionable. The newspaper featured the story of a mother who had reported seeing youths smoking "reefers" at a Derby café. The Borough Medical Officer, Dr V. N. Leyshon, however, claimed that the problem had been "blown out of all proportion". The Mental Health Department, too, claimed the issue had been exaggerated.

Then, in June, the Rev Wynne Lewis, of Elim Pentecostal Church in Curzon Street, and the Rev Alan Warrell, minister of Rose Hill Methodist Church, both of whom had spent several months assisting teenage addicts, had warned they were only reaching "the tip of the iceberg". Mr Warrell had also told the Derby branch of Samaritans that it had been confirmed to him, by a pupil and a teacher, that fifth formers at a Derby school had been selling drugs to children in the form below. "Curiously," noted Albert Street, "nobody apparently thought to tell the education authority about this." An investigation had immediately been launched. While it was clear, from the establishment of the specialist unit, that the Derbyshire police were taking the problem of drug-abuse seriously, Albert Street wondered: "May we hope that the police investigations are aimed more at preventing a trade from developing than in tackling one that exists?"

In September 1967, Derby's trolley bus system, which had been running since 1932, was closed. This picture shows a trolley bus that has reached its destination, the Midland Station.

As if drug issues were not enough, there was great controversy in October when the Derbyshire Education Committee proposed permitting the sale of alcoholic beverages in those Youth Service premises that catered for the over-18s. Their intention was to create a realistic, but guided, introduction into the adult world.

"We are asking our present youth workers to do the impossible in directing young people's thoughts towards mature conditions in an atmosphere characterised by table tennis and soft drinks." The report also pointed out: "Students' Unions have had similar facilities for many years." It also suggested that local traders – not just publicans, but shop owners too – might be allowed, in turn, to take a monthly tenancy in the youth clubs where they could display and sell "books, musical instruments, cosmetics, clothes, sports and photographic equipment and so on" or, in the case of licensees, beer.

A trip to the zoo – or further afield?

FOR entertainment that could be enjoyed by the whole family, there were plenty of helpful advertisements placed in advance of the August Bank Holiday. Twycross Zoo encouraged families to come to see their "new babies", Sultan and Suki the tiger cubs, Simon the puma and Stripes the tapir, as well as everyone's favourite, the chimps' tea party. At Matlock Bath, the Venetian Nights and Grand Illuminations were under way and there was a chance to visit the Heights of Abraham, "the Switzerland of England".

"Staffordshire's greatest stately home", Blithfield Hall, and its neighbouring reservoir were also suggested. For those wanting to venture further afield, Barton's offered regular trips to Skegness, Blackpool and Great Yarmouth, and longer trips to the real Switzerland, Italy and Belgium. The Westminster Bank, which had branches in Irongate and the Cornmarket, asked readers: "Sun seeking this year?" The bank was advertising its currency exchange.

Brian Clough comes to town

ALTHOUGH early results might not have suggested it, the temperature at the Baseball Ground was set to rise. In May came perhaps the most important day in the history of Derby County: the arrival of new manager Brian Clough. With one game remaining of the 1966-67 season, the club had sacked manager Tim Ward, a former Rams and England international, together with trainer Ralph Hann, another former player. Clough, who was just 32 years old, brought with him his former Middlesbrough teammate, Peter Taylor. The Rams' brash new boss promised supporters one thing: that the side would finish higher than their 17th place in the season just ended. In fact, they would finish one place lower, but no one seemed to mind. They could see the enormous changes taking place on the field as Clough swept through the Baseball Ground like a hurricane, never mind a breath of fresh air.

However, one member of the squad was less happy. Twenty-two-year-old goalkeeper, Colin Boulton, who had deputised for the injured Reg Matthews, had been relegated to the reserves once Matthews had recovered. Boulton wanted desperately to play first-team football, and requested a transfer. Fortunately, for Boulton, and for Derby County fans, he would be persuaded

For another sporting local hero, there was disappointment. In June, Swadlincote's Jack Bodell met Henry Cooper for the British and Empire boxing titles at Wolverhampton Wanderers' Molineux Ground, but was stopped in the second round. By contrast, the annual Shrovetide football match at Ashbourne, in which Derby County chairman Sam Longson had thrown up the first ball, had the highest score for 71 years – with three balls played and goaled.

to stay, and the goalkeeper would be the only ever-present in both the Rams' Championship successes in the 1970s.

In September, Derbyshire sports fans mourned the death of the remarkable Harry Storer. He had played football for Derby County and England, and in Derbyshire's County Cricket Championship-winning side of 1936, before returning to the Rams as manager, leading them to the Third Division North title in 1956-57.

1968

Foot and Mouth Disease

BY the beginning of 1968, the spectre of foot and mouth disease had become an unwelcome reality for Derbyshire folk. Both the Peak District and the south of the county were affected, with new cases reported each week. The transport of livestock was limited, sometimes prohibited, through much of the county. Protective measures, such as the closing of roads and the compulsory disinfecting of vehicles and footwear, were introduced and, in a bid to stop the spread of the deadly disease, Peak District wardens guarded roadblocks and stopped walkers traversing the moors. Dozens of local farms were affected – like Church Farm at Morley, where 77 cattle and 80 sheep were afflicted. But, as each area was cleared of infection, stretches of countryside and road were eventually reopened.

More political change

BY the end of March, with the worst of the outbreak over, attention moved to the imminent reorganisation of Derby Borough Council. There was to be a redefinition of its geograph-ical and political boundaries and the absorption of several outlying villages. The expansion increased the population of the borough from around 128,000 residents, to an estimated 200,000 overnight. As the *Evening Telegraph* pointed out, this meant the end for what it described as "a venerable public institution – the parish council".

Not everyone was looking forward to the changes, however. Mr A. A. Matthews, chairman of Chellaston Parish Council, was particularly vociferous in his disapproval. He had repeatedly protested the changes and, at the final meeting of his parish council, had declared that they were about "to become part of that soulless organisation called the Derby Borough".

Largely, however, the changes were accepted as inevitable and necessary, if not ideal. As the *Evening Telegraph* noted: "It speaks volumes for the smooth efficiency and careful nature of Derby's takeover that, broadly speaking, any parish rancour which it engendered has already given way to realistic co-operation and cautious optimism for the future."

With the first election of the new borough approaching, columnist "Albert Street" was less concerned whether Conservative or Labour would control the town, than he was about the level of enthusiasm for voting.

Such "chronic lethargy that, ever since the war, has weakened the town's government and made tales about the 'will of the people' a sick joke" had meant that, at the previous local election, less than one-third of those eligible had bothered to cast their vote.

Parking problems and other traffic controversies

PERHAPS it was party politics that so turned-off Derby voters; there seemed to be plenty of opinions voiced about all manner of issues, from traffic management to environmental matters. Even public parking was causing a stir. In particular, the car park in the Market Place was under scrutiny. Although there were 60 spaces available, "one particular Friday, 53 vehicles stood all day in the car park, leaving only seven spaces to be shared by other drivers". Local businessmen, it seemed, were to blame.

Speeding traffic was causing concern for residents along part of Derby's Ring Road. A petition by residents of Osmaston ward was sent to the Ministry of Transport "in an effort to obtain safety measures for pedestrians on Osmaston Park Road". The Ministry announced that it was reviewing traffic speed limits on the entire Ring Road. Pleas for a subway crossing in the area were ruled out, however, due to budget limits. Osmaston councillor A. M. Baird had been told that there was a possibility that Nightingale Road might be considered for the "new X-way crossing".

Ultimately, of course, this crossing would take the form of the "Spider Bridge" at the junctions of Harvey, Osmaston Park, Osmaston and Chellaston roads.

At the junction of Manor Road-Warwick Avenue and Burton Road, street widening and the installation of traffic lights was proposed. And the new council also promised to create "extensive traffic-free precincts and overhead service roads".

In Mickleover, too, new road building was proving controversial. It had been proposed to create a Littleover-Mickleover bypass between the Derby Ring Road and the A38. A public enquiry considered several proposals, among them one from the Department of Transport that would join the road with the Ring Road near Brackensdale Avenue and rejoin the A38 at Findern, taking traffic away from the congested section of A38 that ran through Littleover.

Part of the link would also take traffic away from the centre of Mickleover. However, the Bishop Lonsdale College of Education at Mickleover would lose some of its grounds to the scheme and had its own proposals for the route of the road. Represented by a civil engineer, the college complained that the route of the road, as outlined by the ministry, showed that the "ministry appeared to assume that the college's playing fields were unimportant and purely recreational".

The college would also have to go to great expense to find additional playing fields and to double-glaze and air condition the entire complex because of an increased noise level that would "interfere with the audibility of a lecturer and the concentration of the students".

However, the college's scheme would necessitate the demolition of 16 houses, rather than the eight anticipated under the ministry plan. Predictably, the college's suggestion that the needs of its 700 students and staff were greater than that of local households, and that the loss of an extra eight houses would be of little concern because local residents would rather leave their homes entirely than live near to a main road, did not prove popular with their neighbours.

Mrs Rawcliffe, representing one householder on Uttoxeter Road, noted: "The ministry's line, from the householder's view is very much more humanitarian than the line proposed by the college." Mr J. W. Best, another Uttoxeter Road resident, called the college suggestion a "callous scheme".

Concerns over a noisy night club ... and an incinerator

RESIDENTS of Melbourne Street, off Normanton Road, were also unhappy. The popular Balmoral Club, on neighbouring Charnwood Street, wanted to extend its premises. Thirty-one householders in Melbourne Street had signed a petition against the proposal. They had already complained about Balmoral patrons parking their cars in their street, so that locals had nowhere to park, and about being woken up in the early hours by noisy clubbers returning to their cars.

In Sunnyhill, there was much controversy over Qualcast's proposed incinerator. Fears that its chimney would emit dirty smoke, in what was now a smokeless zone, seemed of greatest concern. The manufacturers reassured locals that, although it was meant to burn factory waste and paint, the incinerator would emit only water vapour and carbon dioxide – both of which, it was claimed, would benefit trees and gardens. Qualcast also pointed out that the new incinerator would be an improvement on the previous one, and that the new device would comply with the Clean Air Act.

Business is still booming

ANOTHER Derby industry was celebrating success in 1968. Rolls-Royce had been awarded "the most lucrative jet engine contract in the history of commercial aviation", according to the *Evening Telegraph*. The company was to provide its new RB211 engines for aeroplane manufacturer Lockheed for its 1011 Tri-jet airliners. Two of the biggest US airlines – Eastern and Trans World – had ordered the engines to power 50 and 44 aircraft respectively. The contract amounted to around £98 million worth of business. Months of careful negotiation had been needed to persuade the American companies to accept foreign engines in their aircraft. So good was the news that Prime Minister Harold Wilson telephoned Rolls-Royce chief executive Sir Denning Pearson from his retreat at Chequers to congratulate him.

In October, Aiton & Company Ltd obtained an order for the supply and erection of pipe work for the new Sundance thermal power station near Edmonton. It was only the latest in a long line of contracts with Canadian companies.

With business apparently booming, it was not surprising to see that several local businesses were seeking new employees. What may surprise modern Derbeians is the nature of the advertisements – and how gender specific they were allowed to be. Linen Maid Limited of Duffield wanted "women and girls" for evening work. James Smith & Co of Drewry Lane wanted "ladies for employment at machinists". Glow-Worm of Belper required "women and girls for assembly work". Granary Garages, near Burton, wanted a car salesman: "We

Derby Co-operative Society's Peak Bakery business off Osmaston Park Road in this c.1960s aerial view.

are looking for a man with proven motor trade experience." And an "experienced salesman" was needed to "sell unusual product to increasing market. Car supplied" With no clue as to the nature, or name of the business, applicants had to respond to a *Telegraph* box number. Systems Programming Limited, a computer consultancy organisation, were a little more broad in their requirements, even if their advertisement seemed a little twee. With the possibility of working in Europe they wanted "rare birds (male or female!)" that could "fly high".

For those who fancied branching out on their own, a number of small businesses were for sale. A "high class grocery and butchery in the centre of beautiful Derbyshire village, few miles Derby" was available for £12,000, while a general store cost £3,250 and a newsagent's £3,500, all before stock was taken into account.

Stage and screen success

THE entertainment world offered much for Derbeians in 1968. The Playhouse had enjoyed a successful, if low-key, season but the theatre's policy "has fallen more on 'guest' rather than on 'star'". There had been some celebrity performers – Bill Kerr, famous for his roles in *Hancock's Half Hour* and *Compact*, and

Carry On star Bernard Bresslaw. However, noted the *Evening Telegraph,* "most guests have been only from the slightly lower rungs". Touring shows, such as Harry Corbet and his *Sooty Show,* and an appearance by Joyce Grenfell, had supplemented plays.

For those with more trendy tastes, John Peel, "Britain's top disc jockey" made a personal appearance at the Clouds Club in Derby where he "entertained a fair-sized crowd with his own brand of drawling chatter, subtle wit, and a handsome bundle of fresh and interesting records". Travelling with him was his "female singing discovery", Bridgette St John, who caused an "unearthly silence to fall on the club with her four wonderful songs".

A number of Derbyshire entertainers were also making headlines in 1968. Derby-born film and theatre director John Dexter released his cinematic version of Leslie Thomas's *The Virgin Soldiers.* Allestree's Alan Bates celebrated an Oscar nomination for his performance as a Russian Jew jailed for a murder he did not commit, in *The Fixer.* Bates was also busy, with co-stars Oliver Reed and Glenda Jackson, filming D. H. Lawrence's *Women In Love* around the county, and in particular at Kedleston Hall. 1968 also marked the year Hayfield native Arthur Lowe debuted in the role that would define his long career, and immortalise him. *Dad's Army,* featuring the exploits of the Walmington-on-Sea platoon of the Home Guard and their well-meant, if sometimes haphazard, attempts at keeping Britain safe from invasion was to run for 80 episodes over nine series, with the Derbyshire actor playing a central role throughout.

1969

A chilly start ...

THERE appeared little sign of a let-up in the arctic conditions that had heralded the New Year in Derbyshire. Snow fell throughout January 1969, and even as a "mini-thaw" set in around the middle of February, roads in the north of the county remained closed with layers of snow and ice compacted to create treacherous conditions. Derby's own meteorologist, Mr M. Matthews, who had a small weather station at his home on Brayfield Avenue, Littleover, recorded maximum temperatures of 32 degrees Fahrenheit.

For many people, however, what the *Evening Telegraph* called "Peakland's Wintry Mantle" was an opportunity to pursue favourite pastimes. With 11 degrees of frost recorded, the lake at Melbourne froze over, and dozens of ice skaters took full advantage. Some even got out their skis as the county's parks became "impromptu winter sports centres".

The snowfall of 19 February, however, proved less appealing. A remarkable blizzard, which began around lunchtime and lasted until evening rush-hour, made left many roads impassable and driving conditions appalling. By evening, commuters right across the county found many routes home blocked, or under deep drifts of snow, some as deep as ten feet.

A double-decker from the Willington-based Blue Bus Company took well over an hour to turn out of Doles Lane at Findern on to the A38, which was at a standstill from Pastures Hill in Littleover as far back as Lichfield, with lorries jack-knifed along the route.

Regular journeys of minutes took hours, as long processions of cars and buses moved barely above snail's pace. In its 20 February edition, the *Evening Telegraph* reported "conditions as bad as 1947 and worsening by the hour". As more and more snow fell, villages were cut off and motorists forced to spend the night in their stranded cars. Train services were badly affected and Parwich Hospital became isolated from the outside world. It would be several weeks before the last traces of ice would melt away.

Transport rules but there are technical challenges

BY the beginning of February, work had finally begun on the demolition of Devonshire House in the Cornmarket, and precise details of the St Alkmund's Way-Nottingham Road-Siddalls Road section of the Inner Ring Road was revealed, with work expected to begin in the late summer. This particular section would present many technical challenges. As well as motorised traffic, the main Derby to Leeds railway line had to be accommodated. And, because two sections of the complicated road plan would have to be built below the level of the Derwent, "advanced engineering technique" would be employed to prevent problems with water pressure and avoid the possibility of flooding.

Traffic planners revealed plans for a one-way traffic system within the town centre. Some three miles of road were to be converted to one-way traffic, with public transport to be given priority in "to a degree rarely accepted in other busy centres". The planners firmly believed that, as well, as making travel in the town centre less complicated, the one-way system would allow twice as many vehicles to be accommodated on the same roads. There could also be more traffic signals and pedestrian crossings, which would vastly improve traffic flow and pedestrian access. There was also to be a parking meter system installed; and 75,000 free copies of a motorists' guide to Derby would be distributed explaining the new routes, parking restrictions and new car parks "several weeks before the scheme is introduced".

Selling a table? Or moving house?

FOR those Derbeians wanting to replace their old home furnishings, the *Evening Telegraph* "Miscellaneous Sales" advertisements provided an opportunity to clear out unwanted items, while those unable or unwilling to buy brand new items, could find plenty of second-hand bargains.

Someone named Martin, from Milford, was looking to sell a gate leg table (£3 10s), four fireside chairs (£2 10s) and an electric clothes dryer (£3 10s). In Mickleover, an Avalon double-bed settee was available for £30. Other items on offer included a modern fireplace for £5; a gas cooker for £25; and a large asbestos garage with double doors in good condition for £20.

Summer, as always, was a popular time to move house and in August, among the attractive properties for advertised sale by Derby estate agent Frank Innes was a "superbly individual architect designed detached residence" at Quarndon village. A brand new house, it was "nearing completion" and featured antique fireplace and door furniture, as well as a "joiner-made model kitchen". It had four bedrooms, two reception rooms, a breakfast room/playroom, kitchen, cloakroom, and a detached brick double garage. It cost a whopping £13,450.

Another featured property was a detached cottage at Kirk Ireton, due for auction the following month. "With one picture," the agent declared, "we cannot do justice to this beautifully converted and modernised stone built ... cottage". At Darley Abbey, Frank Innes offered an "architecturally designed" detached house "built to a high quality specification in first class situation overlooking Darley Park". There was a lounge, dining room, breakfast room, kitchen with stainless steel sink unit, storeroom, larder, three double bedrooms, bathroom, WC and a detached matching garage and lovely gardens: all for £7,500.

At Ashbourne "the Gateway to Dovedale" there was a "superior detached residence" with a long hall and large lounge with a dining area off, "exceptionally well equipped kitchen", a ground floor cloakroom, three good-sized bedrooms and an "expensively equipped bathroom". This particular house, its garage and garden, could be purchased for £6,850. For less ambitious homeowners, an end-of terrace house on Crewe

Street was available for £1,200, and a "fully modernised very well equipped two-bedroomed terrace house" could be one lucky Derby family's for just £1,595.

Hostile demonstrations

EVEN in Derby there was no protection from the controversies and troubles of the nation. For some time there had been much anger and debate at the racist perspective of Conservative MP Enoch Powell, who had made a speech warning of troubles should Britain continue its policy of allowing immigration from the Commonwealth, and even suggesting that "urgent encouragement of re-emigration" should take place.

His own party leader, Edward Heath, had removed Powell from his shadow cabinet, declaring he was "liable to exacerbate racial tensions". It was unsurprising, then, that Powell's appearance at the Gold Mine bingo hall in Chaddesden in May was met with what the *Evening Telegraph* called "hostile demonstrators". Members of the Indian Workers' Association, from Derby and Nottingham, were joined, the paper noted, "by Communist Party members and other left-wingers".

Police officers, who "must have outnumbered demonstrators", did not allow protesters inside, there was "no violence". But then police received word that there was a bomb in the building and had no choice but to clear the area. People who had taken their seats in advance of the meeting of the South-East Derbyshire Conservative Association were politely asked to leave "in an orderly manner".

After a full search, the threat was found to be a hoax and the meeting went ahead, with Powell being driven to the entrance from the Chaddesden Park Hotel where he had been attending a reception. There were brief interruptions from "hecklers" who had managed to get into the meeting despite the police presence, but bomb threats aside, the speech passed off without incident.

Christmas preparations, even for thieves

ALTHOUGH the end of the year saw the county anticipating a new decade, for most Derbeians celebrations concentrated on a traditional Christmas, rather than New Year. Even criminals, it seemed, were preparing for the festivities. In mid-December "pre-Christmas raiders stocked up with good things at the expense of two Derby shops and a club", the *Evening Telegraph* reported. More than £150 worth of cigarettes was stolen from the Gower Street shop of Mr John Watts, and spirits, wine, cigarettes and chocolates were taken from the Balaclava Road branch of the Derby Co-operative Society. Even the Derbyshire Lawn Tennis Association Club in Stanton Street was broken into, with bottles of wine stolen. Houses, too, fell victim, including a bungalow near Normanton Park, from which a transistor radio and electricity meter money had been taken. And another mini crime wave had seen no less than 11 schools broken into since September.

For those choosing to acquire their festive goodies legally, the Co-op placed a full-page "Christmas Fare" advertisement in the *Evening Telegraph*. Norfolk Manor turkeys for 4s 4d per pound, while "Prime English Pork" was 5s 2d per pound. There were Robirch pork pies of various sizes, "Australian Fruits", Co-op table jellies for 7d, mincemeat for 1s 7d, dairy cream for 1s 1d, and Christmas Yule Logs for 5s 5d. For feline friends Kit-e-Kat was on offer of three cans for 2s 2d. "Softy" bread, which "keeps freshest longest", was also on offer with tips from one the country's bakery experts on how to keep it edible for even longer still.

For some families, Christmas parties would have to be postponed: Derbyshire was in the grip of a 'flu epidemic. Shops and offices, schools and factories were affected. By the end of December, the situation had become so grim that local hospitals were forced to appeal for volunteers "particularly ex-nurses", as doctors, domestics and more than 100 nurses in the main hospitals were off work with 'flu. All non-urgent admissions to main hospitals were postponed. Pastures Hospital at Mickleover had lost a quarter of its female workers. Local bus services, too, had been hit by illness and the Carriage and Wagon Works was experiencing higher than usual absenteeism.

With Christmas Day falling on a Thursday in 1969, there were no deliveries over the entire weekend, and by Monday an "unprecedented" demand for 'flu drugs had meant that several Derby chemists had run out of supplies of tetracycline antibiotics. A number of Derbeians had endured fruitless tours around local chemists in an attempt at getting stricken relatives' prescriptions fulfilled, before giving up and leaving their orders in the hope that the medicine would be available later in the day. Only as the New Year arrived, and Derbyshire looked forward to the 1970s, would conditions improve.